Paintings, Watercolors, Drawings and Sculpture

collected by

Mr. and Mrs. Ralph F. Colin

Pamela T. Colin and Ralph F. Colin, Jr.

(*Frontispiece*) MATISSE Jeune Fille en vert à la Fenêtre (*Girl in Green*) No. 18

THE
COLIN COLLECTION

Paintings, Watercolors, Drawings and Sculpture

collected by

MR. & MRS. RALPH F. COLIN

PAMELA T. COLIN & RALPH F. COLIN, JR.

New York

M. KNOEDLER & COMPANY

NEW YORK

THE COLIN COLLECTION

WAS EXHIBITED AT THE KNOEDLER GALLERY

IN NEW YORK FROM APRIL 12 TO MAY 14, 1960

FOR THE BENEFIT OF THE HOSPITALIZED VETERANS

SERVICE OF THE MUSICIANS' EMERGENCY FUND

Library of Congress Catalogue Card Number 60-9553

Printed in England by W. S. Cowell Ltd at their Press
in the Butter Market, Ipswich

FOREWORD *by James Thrall Soby*

What strikes one forcefully about the collection of Mr. and Mrs. Colin is its exceptional range of sensitivity. They have been able to appreciate and cherish the proto-expressionist vehemence of Daumier's sculpture and the transcendental calm of Arp's, the tragic sobriety of Rouault no less than the gaiety of Klee and Miró, the humility of Vuillard and Morandi as much as the passion of Modigliani, the classicism of Gris and the ferociousness of Soutine. One senses, too, in reviewing the dates when the Colins' acquisitions were made, that their taste has broadened and enriched itself steadily since they began to collect some twenty-odd years ago. At first they tended to prefer works of art with a strong emotional content, painted with rich impasto; Soutine and Rouault were particular favorites. But with time they have acquired a heartening flexibility of judgment, while surrendering nothing of that qualitative strictness which is the gift of all true connoisseurs.

Like an encouraging number of American collectors in this generation, the Colins have a far more diligent and scholarly approach to their avocation than was common here in earlier times. Their art library is extensive and carefully planned, they comb the galleries here and abroad with energy, they bring to their purchases not only instinctive flair, but comparative standards which allow them often to recognize quality within quality, that is, to pick outstanding works by outstanding men. As a result, their collection abounds in such absolute jewels as Matisse's *Guitariste*, to mention only one among many examples. Moreover, their perception has not become frozen in time, as happens frequently even to collectors of decided talent. If their first love was for the giants of the original School of Paris, they now have an eager regard for some of the best younger painters and sculptors. Their group of Dubuffets is a case in point. Not only is it one of the largest in any public or private collection, but it summarizes handsomely the various facets of Dubuffet's major contribution to the art of the post-war period.

The very size of the Colins' collection of Dubuffets points up another characteristic of their estimable taste. Their appetite for the works of an artist they admire does not let them off easily; they must go on buying until at last their hunger abates, though often only temporarily. Of the art of Vuillard, Matisse, Rouault, Picasso, Gris and Soutine they own multiple examples, and these in their private hours of meditation are pitted one against the other with affectionate intensity and discrimination. Moreover, it must be noted, again in contrast to numerous American collectors of previous generations, that the Colins' excitement is by no means reserved for what used to be called, vaingloriously, the hand-painted oil. They have always had a deep interest in watercolors, drawings and prints, and sculpture holds an important place in their collection, which includes admirable pieces by men as different as Brancusi, Despiau, Degas, Giacometti, Lipchitz, Marini, Matisse, Moore, Rodin and the astonishingly talented younger Britisher, Reg Butler. In consequence the collection has a depth and variety not often come upon in this era of sometimes unthinking or intolerant specialization. And quality ties it together without strain.

Now for a while the Colin collection will be on public view. Those who have seen it many times in their home will await the event as eagerly as those never before thus privileged.

NEW CANAAN

April 1960

INTRODUCTION *by Ralph F. Colin*

The works represented in this catalogue have been collected over a period of about twenty-five years. Many of them which today appear safe and "stylish" have only been recognized as the works of twentieth-century masters since we acquired them. In the thirties, they appeared to many of our friends as strange and controversial as do the abstract expressionist works today. The moral is clear – the artists point the way and we, the relatively educated public, follow at a slower pace. Not that everything which is not readily comprehended is "art"; but little that is immediately and universally accepted is likely to have the staying power required of a work which has lasting merit and appeal.

The collection has been made not only by my wife and myself but also by our son and daughter, now in their twenties. Early in their childhood they joined us in our interest in art, stimulated by our offer that they could each choose a painting of their own. They have ever since been the proud possessors of those first choices – Pamela the Soutine *Alley of Trees* (number 89) and Ralph, Jr. the Soutine *Portrait of a Boy in Blue* (number 86), and have subsequently acquired many other paintings, drawings and sculptures by gift and their own purchase.

This group of paintings and sculptures is not truly a collection in any formal sense. It does not represent a cross-section of a period or type of art. Many outstanding artists of the period are not represented at all, some others are sparsely represented, others represented perhaps to excess. But we were not under the obligations of a museum to be either fair or broad-minded. We bought only what my wife and I both liked. When we had the funds we bought what was then available. Under this system we missed many worthwhile works. For instance, my wife appreciated Klee much earlier than I did and we acquired our first Klee only when I shared her enthusiasm – too late to get many choice works before the prices were beyond us. But, at least, everything we ever bought we both liked – and still do, in varying degrees.

In one way this collection differs from many, in that it still includes every work, except one painting, ever acquired by us. One Soutine was traded toward the acquisition of a more important Soutine which was offered to us at a time when we did not have all the cash needed for its purchase. But aside from that all the "mistakes" remain. We know, of course, that all of the works are not of equal importance or artistic merit;

and yet we have repeatedly found it impossible to part with any of them – even toward the acquisition of something else we badly wanted but could not afford. Each of them has come to mean something definite and individual to us, and parting with any one of them would be a real loss. To this extent we have admittedly adjusted our critical faculties.

Collecting has given us all great pleasure, a pleasure we continue to enjoy. Even my task of preparing this catalogue, which I managed between the demands of a busy professional life, has added to that pleasure. For the checking of provenances I am deeply grateful to Mr. Helmut Ripperger and his admirable staff of librarians at M. Knoedler & Company, but whatever faults and errors this catalogue may disclose are chargeable only to me.

Especial thanks are expressed here to the Art Division of the New York Public Library, the librarians and staffs of The Frick Art Reference Library, the Library of The Metropolitan Museum of Art, and the Library of The Museum of Modern Art, New York; all of whom have been unsparing in giving of their knowledge and their time.

A word about art dealers. We are happy to acknowledge that we have learned much from such dealers as Pierre Matisse, Georges Keller, Roland Balaÿ, Sam Salz, the late Curt Valentin, and Valentine Dudensing, now retired and living in France. Not only have they, and others, taught us much but they have become our very good friends. Without such stimulating dealers I believe there would be fewer collectors, and certainly fewer self-supporting artists.

I am grateful to all the critics and writers from whose works I have quoted; especially to Alfred A. Barr, Jr., Andrew Carnduff Ritchie, James Thrall Soby and Monroe Wheeler, who have generously permitted me to quote at such length from their many publications for The Museum of Modern Art. I am specially indebted to Jean Dubuffet who graciously permitted me to publish in my notes to some of his paintings (numbers 92 to 98) quotations from his own notes for a lecture, a copy of which he gave to my wife some years ago; to Rufino Tamayo who wrote for this catalogue the statement of his artistic credo which appears as a comment to his recent *Children's Games* (number 91); and to René d'Harnoncourt who at my request translated Tamayo's statement from the Spanish. And, finally, I am more than grateful to Jim Soby not only for being willing to fit into his busy writing schedule the preparation of the Foreword to this catalogue, but also for the grace and warmth of his comments.

NEW YORK CITY

April 1960

PAINTINGS, WATERCOLORS AND DRAWINGS

1832–1883	EDOUARD MANET	1	Le Petit Lange
1864–1941	ALEXEI VON JAWLENSKY	2	Landscape
		3	Variation, Summer
		4	Variation
1867–1947	PIERRE BONNARD	5	Rue Tholozé
		6	La Bouteille de Vin Rouge
1868–1940	EDOUARD VUILLARD	7	Nature Morte à la Pomme
		8	Still Life with Onions and Knife
		9	Woman in an Interior (*Vuillard's Mother*)
		10	Girl at Window
		11	Self-portrait, Le Canotier
		12	Ma Grand'mère
		13	La Famille Vuillard au Déjeuner
		14	Portrait of the Painter Roussel
		15	Symphonie en Rouge
1869–1954	HENRI MATISSE	16	Guitariste
		17	La Gandoura Verte (*The Green Gandoura Robe*)
		18	Jeune Fille en vert à la Fenêtre (*Girl in Green*)
		19	Odalisques
		20	Reclining Figure
		21	Resting Model
		22	Head of a Girl
1871–1956	LYONEL FEININGER	23	Yellow Village Church III
		24	Paris: Seine at Night
		25	Sunset with Blue Area
1871–1958	GEORGES ROUAULT	26	Head of a Workman (*Head of Christ?*)
		27	The Blue Angel
		28	The Judge
		29	Bouquet
		30	Mille et une Nuit
		31	Girl with Turban

1891–	KARL KNATHS	69	Copper Kettle
1893–	JOAN MIRÓ	70	Au Cirque
		71	La Poétesse
		72	Le Reveil au Petit Jour (*Awakening at Dawn*)
		73	Personages and Star
1894–1943	CHAIM SOUTINE	74	Still Life with Soup Tureen
		75	Still Life with Cabbage
		76	Peasant Boy
		77	Landscape at Céret
		78	Gnarled Trees
		79	Gladiolas
		80	The Apprentice
		81	Landscape at Cagnes
		82	Side of Beef
		83	Landscape at Vence
		84	White House on a Hill
		85	Le Garçon d'Etage (*The Floor Waiter*)
		86	Portrait of Boy in Blue
		87	Female Nude
		88	Fish
		89	Alley of Trees
1899–	RUFINO TAMAYO	90	Portrait of Olga
		91	Children's Games
1901–	JEAN DUBUFFET	92	Mouleuse de Café (*The Coffee-Grinder*)
		93	Grande Vue de Paris
		94	Histoires Naturelles
		95	Tête au Teint de Sucre (*Head with Sugar Complexion*)
		96	Tête au Nez Lilas (*Head with Lilac Nose*)
		97	La Montagne Rose (*The Rose Mountain*)
		98	Vache à l'Herbage (*Cow in Pasture*)
		99	Femme à la Fourrure (*Woman with Furs*)
		100	African Landscape
1905–	FRITZ WINTER	101	Mit Gelb (*With Yellow*)
		102	Linear Blau (*Linear Blue*)
1910–	MORRIS GRAVES	103	Woodpecker
1919–	PIERRE SOULAGES	104	Painting – 6 March 55
1923–	JEAN-PAUL RIOPELLE	105	Dérive
		106	Brumaire

SCULPTURES

The Catalogue

The Catalogue is arranged chronologically in the order of the dates of birth of the artists; paintings, watercolors and drawings appear first in one sequence of items 1 through 106, and sculptures thereafter in a second sequence of items 107 through 132.

In the text the date is enclosed in brackets when it does not appear on the work.

All dimensions of paintings and drawings are in inches; height precedes width. For the sculpture, the nature of the dimensions is stated in each case.

Titles appear in the form in which the work has been best known. Translations or alternate titles appear only where they seem desirable.

References appear in full under "References". However, in the footnotes and elsewhere in identifying quotations, the following frequent references are abbreviated as indicated:

BARR, *Matisse:*	Alfred H. Barr, Jr., *Matisse: His Art and His Public*, New York, The Museum of Modern Art, 1951.
BARR, *Picasso:*	Alfred H. Barr, Jr., *Picasso, Fifty Years of His Art*, New York, The Museum of Modern Art, 1946.
RITCHIE, *Vuillard:*	Andrew Carnduff Ritchie, *Edouard Vuillard*, New York, The Museum of Modern Art, 1954.
SOBY, *Arp:*	*Arp*, New York, The Museum of Modern Art, 1958, edited with an introduction by James Thrall Soby and with articles by Jean Hans Arp, Richard Huelsenbeck, Robert Melville, Carola Giedion-Welcker.
SOBY, *Gris:*	James Thrall Soby, *Juan Gris*, New York, The Museum of Modern Art, 1958.
SOBY, *Rouault:*	James Thrall Soby, *Georges Rouault: Paintings and Prints*, New York, The Museum of Modern Art (1945), 3rd Edition, 1947.
WHEELER, *Soutine:*	Monroe Wheeler, *Soutine*, New York, The Museum of Modern Art, 1950.

Illustrations in Color

Of the twelve illustrations in color appearing on the pages which follow, those numbered below were reproduced originally in books published by The Museum of Modern Art, New York, and by Editions d'Art Albert Skira, Geneva, to whom grateful acknowledgment is made:

Numbers 29, 58, 59, 71, 86, 89 *The Museum of Modern Art*

Numbers 5, 19, 43, 51 *Editions d'Art Albert Skira*

No. 5 BONNARD Rue Tholozé

No. 16 MATISSE Guitariste

No. 19 MATISSE Odalisques

No. 29 ROUAULT Bouquet

No. 55 MODIGLIANI Nu au Collier (*Nude with Necklace*)

No. 51 BRAQUE Céret: The Rooftops

No. 43 PICASSO Vase de Fleurs

No. 58 GRIS Violon et Guitare

No. 59 GRIS Livre, Pipe et Verres (*Book, Pipe and Glasses*)

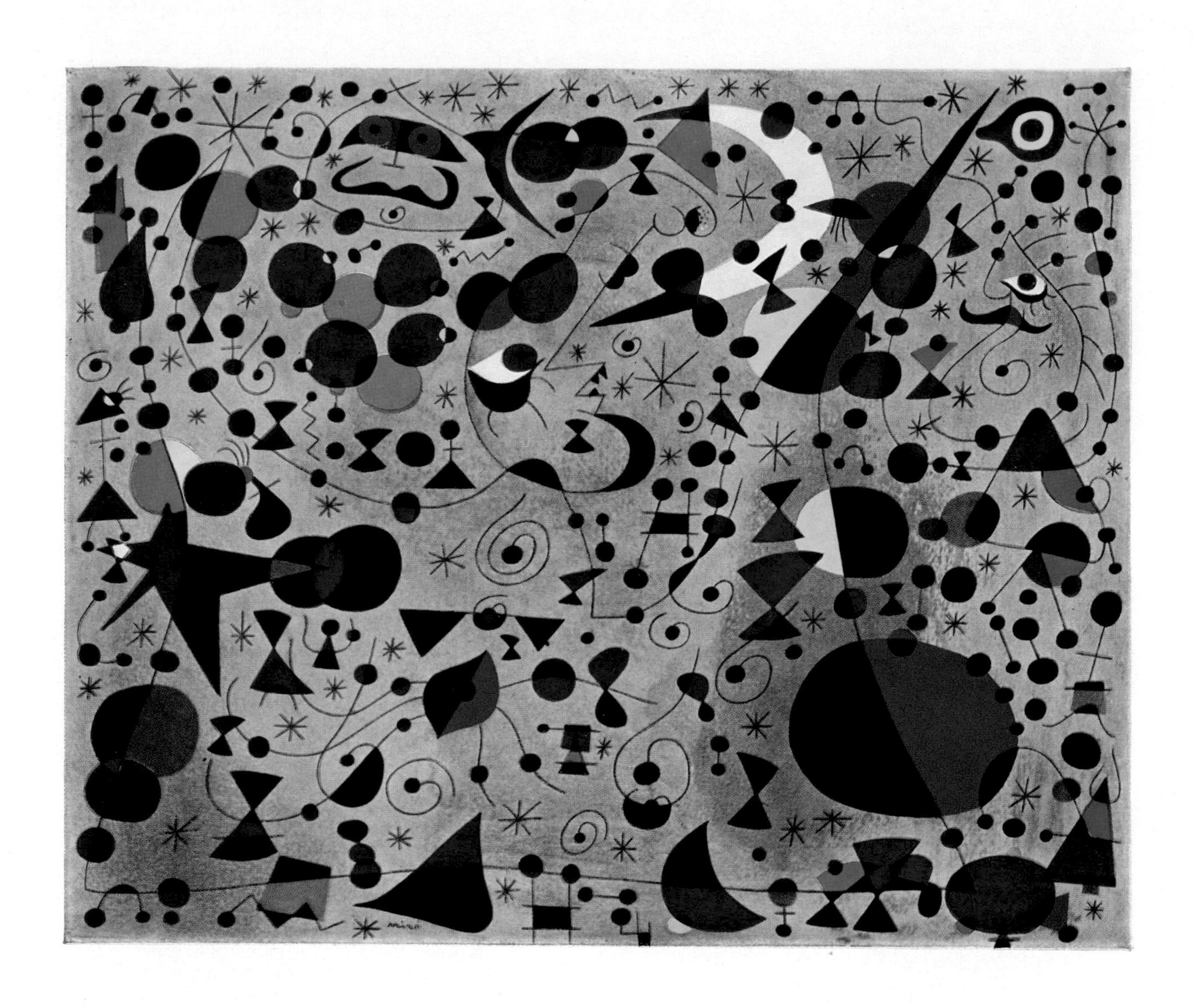

No. 71 MIRÓ La Poétesse

No. 86 SOUTINE Portrait of Boy in Blue

No. 89 SOUTINE Alley of Trees

Illustrations in Black and White

Edouard Manet 1832–1883

1 LE PETIT LANGE

Oil on canvas, 46 × 28

(1861–62)

Signed lower right, "ed. Manet" *and inscribed* "à Mme. H. Lange"

In 1856, Manet had haunted the museums in The Hague, Amsterdam, Dresden, Munich and Vienna, and then in Florence, Rome and Venice. But although Manet did not actually visit Spain until August of 1865, it was the influence of the Spanish masters which appeared first in his paintings. Not only the subject matter of such works as "The Spanish Guitar-Player", "The Spanish Ballet", "Lola de Valence", "Young Woman in Spanish Costume", "Young Man in the Costume of a Majo" and "The Dead Toreador" (all done before 1865) but also the manner of painting evidence Manet's regard for the Spaniards – especially Velasquez.[1] That regard for a tradition appears clearly in this portrait of the Lange boy done in 1861–62.

Traditional – almost "old-masterly" – as these paintings appear to us today, they were refused at the Salons and ridiculed when shown at a private pavilion at Place de l'Alma during the Paris World's Fair in 1867. It was reported that "Husbands drove their wives up to the Pont de l'Alma. Feeling it was too fine an opportunity to pass up, they came to treat themselves and their families to a good laugh. Every 'self-respecting' painter in Paris turned up at the Manet Exhibition. They all went wild with laughter. . . . All the papers without exception followed their lead."[2] But those times, too, had their Alfred Barrs. Zola wrote : "Our fathers laughed at Monsieur Courbet, and today we go into ecstasies over him. We laugh at Monsieur Manet; it will be our sons who go into ecstasies over his canvases."[3] Because of such views, Zola was discharged as an art critic.

While Manet's painting, like that of all truly great artists, was grounded in tradition, we now discern in Manet "the transition from narrative, anecdotal painting to pure painting – 'patches, colors, movement' . . . Unmistakable hints appear in the work of Chardin, Delacroix, Courbet, Turner . . . But Manet was the first to practice the art of painting taken for itself alone, what we call today 'modern painting' . . . With Manet began the repudiation of 'all values foreign to painting', the indifference to the meaning of the subject".[4]

[1] Georges Bataille, *Manet*, New York 1953, page 50. [2] *ibid*, page 10. [3] *ibid*, page 10, quoted from *L'Evenement* of May 1, 1866. [4] *ibid*, page 50.

Collection: Presented by the artist to Mme. Lange; Thannhauser Gallery, Munich; Paul von Bleichert, Leipzig; Mueller, Solothurn; Howard Young Galleries, New York; Mrs. Louis L. Coburn, Chicago; The Art Institute of Chicago.

Exhibited: Ausstellung der Modernen Galerie Heinrich Thannhauser, Munich 1916, described and reproduced in the catalogue page 17; *Loan Exhibition of Manet*, Wildenstein Galleries, New York, February 26–April 3, 1948, number 12, reproduced in the catalogue page 22.

References: Edouard Manet, by Julius Meier-Graefe, Munich 1912, mentioned page 112, reproduced page 113, figure 58; *Der Cicerone*, May 1, 1913, page 321, figure 20; *Katalog der Modernen Galerie Heinrich Thannhauser München*, Munich 1916, reproduced in heliogravure following page 16; *Histoire de Edouard Manet et de son Oeuvre*, by Théodore Duret, Paris 1919, catalogued page 229, number 4; *Manet* by A. Tabarant, Paris 1931, catalogued page 89, number 59; *Manet*, by Jamot, Wildenstein, and Bataille, Paris 1932, catalogued volume 1, page 124, number 72, reproduced volume 2, plate 44, figure 113; *Edouard Manet*, by Paul Colin, Paris 1932, plate VIII (detail); *Meisterwerke europäischer Malerei in Amerika*, by Hans Tietze, Vienna 1935, plate 284; *The Significant Moderns*, by C. J. Bulliet, New York 1936, plate 274; *Masterpieces of European Painting in America*, by Hans Tietze, New York 1939, plate 284; *Art Digest*, February 15, 1944, reproduced page 22; *Notable Paintings including an Important Portrait by Manet*, New York, March 2, 1944, catalogued number 57, reproduced in the catalogue facing page 42; *Manet et ses Oeuvres*, by A. Tabarant, Paris 1947, catalogued page 58, reproduced page 604, figure 61; *The Christian Science Monitor*, February 28, 1948, reproduced page 4.

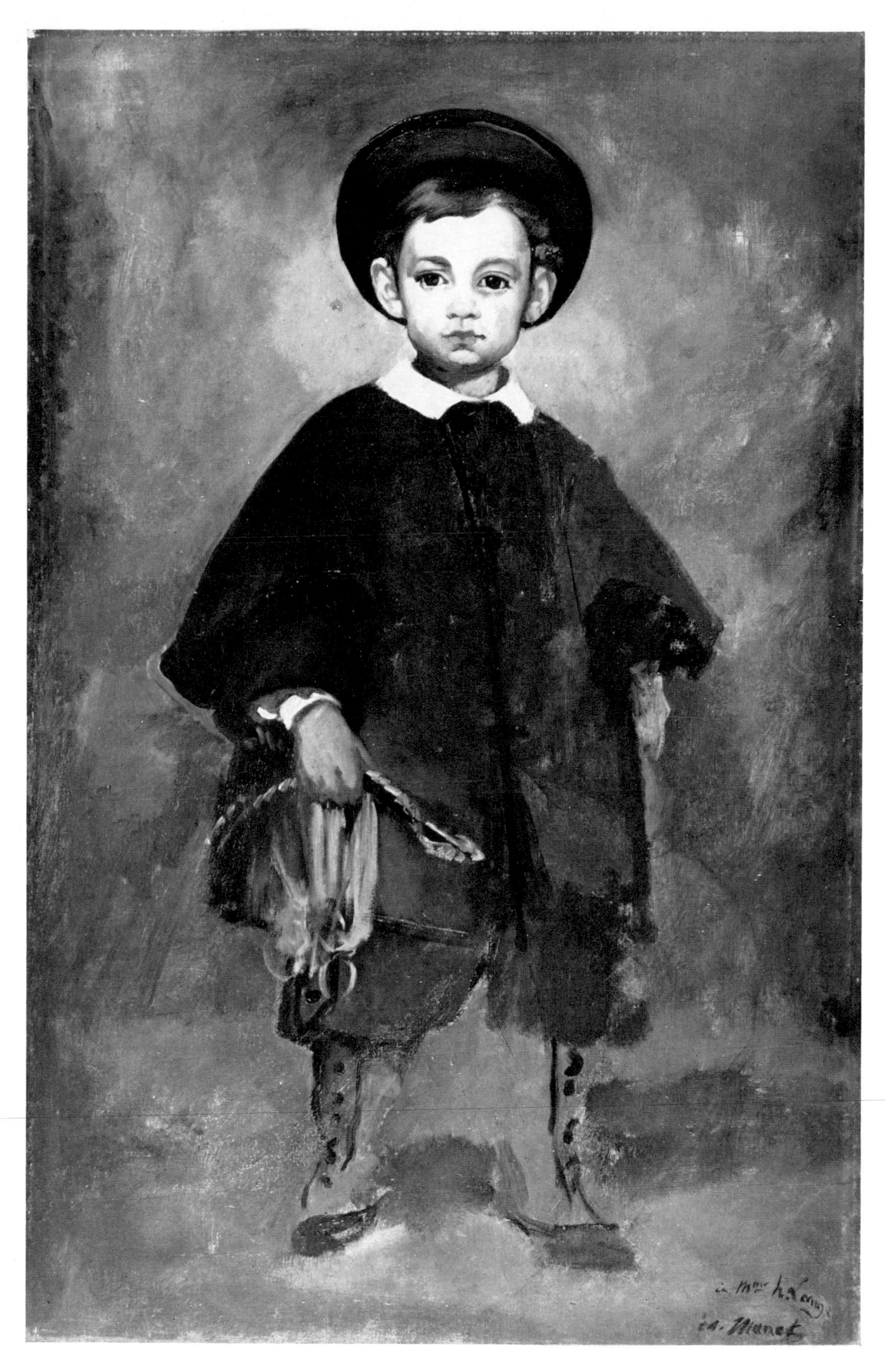

1

Alexei von Jawlensky 1864-1941

2 LANDSCAPE

Oil on board, 13 × 16½

(1910)

Signed lower right, "A Jawlensky"

In the first decade of the twentieth century, a number of Russians constituted the center of a group of artists who settled in the vicinity of Munich. "In 1908 Kandinsky and Gabriele Muenter acquired a house in Murnau; at the same time Jawlensky moved there with Marianna von Werefkin. They had gained an insight into the fluxible situation of painting everywhere by their long journeys throughout Europe and extended stays in Paris. But in Murnau, where they would look at the great range of the mountains, and lived so close to the beloved waters of Lake Staffel, here in the pleasant foothills of the Bavarian Alps, everything learnable and sought after seemed to be forgotten. . . . It is true that Matisse influenced them indirectly through his emancipation of colour. But these darksome landscapes that were now painted with such verve by Kandinsky, Muenter and Jawlensky are in their naïveté, their brilliant freshness, their simplicity and depth, certainly original creations. They launched the march for the *Blaue Reiter* . . . Areas of stronger, deeper colour outlined in black represent mountains, fields, trees, and houses. The brush technique is fast and relaxed, often refreshingly carefree; the pictures seemed improvised, like inspirations of the moment. The character of these landscapes is determined not by the compact instrumentation of the usual palette, not by endless nuances of light and shade, the variety of foliage, grass, and branches, but by the harmony of penetrating tones not so dependent on sculptural factors, and by clearer form accents." (Hans Konrad Roethel, *Modern German Painting*, New York, n.d. pages 27–28.)

Collection: Curt Valentin Gallery, New York.

Exhibited: Der Blaue Reiter, Curt Valentin Gallery, New York, December 7, 1954 – January 8, 1955, number 5; *Artists of the Blaue Reiter*, Busch-Reisinger Museum, Harvard University, January 21 – February 24, 1955, number 6; *Closing Exhibition*, Curt Valentin Gallery, New York, June 1955, number 48.

2

Alexei von Jawlensky 1864-1941

3 VARIATION, SUMMER

Oil on board, 14 × 10¾

(1915)

Signed lower left, "A. J."

The First World War broke up the *Blaue Reiter* group and sent Jawlensky to Switzerland where he remained until 1921. "There he dropped many of his artistic contacts as time went on and took refuge in an increasingly mystical and religious outlook, an attitude not altogether inconsistent with his background.

"As early as 1917 in Switzerland, this transition from the pre-war sensually colored forms to his post-war mystical orientation had become apparent. A batch of delicately tinted landscapes called *Variations*, done on Lake Geneva, was followed by a series of mystic heads, Saviour faces, and finally abstract heads. His often-repeated saying that 'Art is longing for God,' became the *Leitmotiv* for the rest of his work." (Bernard S. Myers, *The German Expressionists*, New York 1956, page 254.)

Collection: Curt Valentin Gallery, New York.

Exhibited: Der Blaue Reiter, Curt Valentin Gallery, New York, December 7, 1954–January 8, 1955, number 9; *Artists of the Blaue Reiter*, Busch-Reisinger Museum, Harvard University, January 21–February 24, 1955, number 10; *Closing Exhibition*, Curt Valentin Gallery, New York, June 1955, number 50.

4 VARIATION

Oil on board, 14½ × 11

(1915)

Unsigned

Collection: Curt Valentin Gallery, New York.

3

4

Pierre Bonnard 1867-1947

5 RUE THOLOZE

Oil on canvas, $25\frac{1}{2} \times 13$

(1917)

Signed lower left, "Bonnard"

" 'Remember that a painting – before being a war-horse, a naked woman, some anecdote or whatnot – is essentially a flat surface covered with colours arranged in a certain order.' This was published on August 23, 1890, in the review *Art et Critique* and signed 'Pierre Louis' (Denis' pseudonym). All Pierre Bonnard's work bears out this *dictum* but, in putting it into practice, he adapted it to the moods of a very personal sensibility, and, as we can see, allowed himself great latitude in the application of its last word, 'order'."[1]

". . . . Bonnard set out to capture in his work what no other painter of his time had observed: the little incidents of Parisian life, the things of which nobody seems to be aware because they repeat themselves continually and constitute in their endless repetition the common elements of daily life. It took the eye of a poetic explorer to be attracted by what everybody saw and eventually even ceased to see because it was neither new nor unusual. Pissarro was beginning to paint the boulevards, the Seine quais and the bridges, seen through his windows, but Bonnard descended into the streets and the squares, watching with equal interest, people, horses, dogs and trees.

"If there exists such a thing as the exquisiteness of banality, that was exactly what Bonnard discovered. Or would it be more correct to say that nothing is banal in itself but that it takes an artist like Bonnard to make us conscious of the wasted charm which surrounds us? His sensibilities were stirred by the awkward grace of a girl carrying a laundry basket through an empty street, by the tired look of a cab-horse on a busy boulevard, by the patter of children's feet hurrying to school, by reddened faces under umbrellas in a snowdrift, by dogs assembling at street corners, by people browsing before an antique shop, by the characteristic movements of women bustling across a street. Cobblestones and monotonous façades, huddled roofs and old walls contributed their delicate coloration, their hidden poetry; broad avenues, busy street vendors, cafés on sidewalks offered him their intricate patterns, their noisy agitation."[2]

[1] Maurice Raynal, *History of Modern Painting: From Baudelaire to Bonnard*, Geneva 1949, page 101. [2] John Rewald, *Pierre Bonnard*, New York 1948, pages 25–6.

Collection: Bernheim-Jeune, Paris; Rosengart, Lucerne; Max Moos, Geneva.

Exhibited: Exposition Pierre Bonnard, Galerie Georges Moos, Zürich, February 4-27, 1947, number 6; *Pierre Bonnard*, The Cleveland Museum of Art, March 2–April 11, 1948, and The Museum of Modern Art, New York, May 10–September 6, 1948, number 33a; *Mid-Century Perspective*, Perls Galleries, New York, January 3–28, 1950, number 2; *Works of Art Belonging to Alumnae*, Smith College Museum of Art, Northampton, Massachusetts, May–June 1950, number 40; *New York Private Collections*, The Museum of Modern Art, New York, June 26–September 12, 1951, number 18.

References: Bonnard, by Gustave Coquiot, Paris 1922, page 49, plate 28; compare a later (1927) and sketchier version of the same subject, reproduced in color in *L'Art d'Aujourd'hui*, Autumn 1927, page 54; "Pierre Bonnard Today", by Daniel Theote, *Tricolor*, April 1944, reproduced page 87; *Bonnard, Peintre du Merveilleux*, Pierre Courthion, Lausanne 1945, reproduced page 61; *Art News*, June-July–August 1948, reproduced page 19; *Pierre Bonnard*, by Gotthard Jedlicka, Erlenbach-Zürich 1949, reproduced facing page 128; *Montmartre*, by Pierre Courthion, Geneva 1956, reproduced in color page 84.

5

Pierre Bonnard 1867-1947

6 LA BOUTEILLE DE VIN ROUGE

Oil on canvas, 26 × 24

1942

Signed lower right, "Bonnard 42"

"When Fauvism was succeeded by Cubism, when Picasso began to emerge as the leading spirit, the most audacious, the most inventive innovator, Bonnard showed himself completely unaffected. His nature dictated another course, one which now began to draw him towards those against whom there had been a revolution in his youth, the Impressionists. If he avoided the brutality with which the *Fauves* and the Cubists deliberately altered the face of the world, his courage was no less than theirs. They often exhibited an intellectual courage while his was a visual one, unconcerned with blasting traditions but always ready to discover with innocent eyes and perpetual astonishment new aspects of forms and new relations of colors. Thus, in his own way, he extended, as they did, the limits of the impossible. He lacked neither boldness nor imagination but he endeavored to express these within the framework of a heritage which he himself broadened to the extent of his needs . . .[1]

". . . . And in spite of all the knowledge accumulated over more than fifty years, his art sprang less from things he had learned than from the ones he carried within himself, from his ability to absorb the spectacle of nature and to re-create it according to the logic of his imagination. He continued to observe incessantly, and for him to observe still meant to enjoy. But there was more than mere enjoyment behind his art, more than just subtlety, good nature and sometimes humor. He achieved the power of those who devote all their abilities to a unique goal, and the serenity that eventually crowns single-minded effort. The works of his last years are not inferior to his early ones in freshness and spontaneity, but their horizon is broadened and their color more intense than ever before. Bonnard gradually extended the gamut of his colorations while at the same time he carried his forms closer to abstraction."[2]

[1] John Rewald, *Pierre Bonnard,* New York 1948, page 42.
[2] *ibid,* page 55.

Collection: Terrasse (heirs of Bonnard, Paris); Sam Salz, New York.

Exhibited: Grands Peintres Contemporains, Nice, April–May 1946, number 1 (lent by Bonnard himself); *New York Private Collections,* The Museum of Modern Art, New York, June 26 – September 12, 1951, number 19; *Loan Exhibition of Paintings by Pierre Bonnard,* Paul Rosenberg & Co., New York, March 12–April 7, 1956, number 21, reproduced in the catalogue page 18.

6

Edouard Vuillard 1868-1940

7 NATURE MORTE A LA POMME

Oil on canvas, $12\frac{1}{2} \times 16$

(1887–88)

Signed lower right, "E. Vuillard"

Vuillard's ". . . first painting of the years 1887–90 are more sensitive to atmosphere and texture than the academic realism of the schools. But they are still very conservative in drawing and restrained in color, by Nabi standards." (They) ". . . suggest an early admiration for Degas, one that was to continue all his life and was, in fact, reciprocated by the older painter. The still lifes of these early years are usually studies of fruit, flowers and bottles. They show a precise delicacy of perception and a sobriety of composition that remind one of Fantin-Latour, Chardin and possibly Vermeer. There are indications, too, especially in the brushwork of some of these still lifes, that he had studied Manet and the Impressionists and also Cézanne. The influence of the latter he may have acquired through his Nabi admiration for Cézanne's disciple, Gauguin. But he was at this time still a student, absorbing from a variety of sources whatever technical means he could." (Ritchie, *Vuillard*, page 10.)

Collection: Jacques Roussel (nephew of the artist), Paris; Sam Salz, New York.

Exhibited: Exposition E. Vuillard, Musée des Arts Décoratifs, Paris, May–July 1938, number 5 as "Bocal de cornichons et pomme", dated 1887–88 and lent by the artist; *Vuillard,* The Cleveland Museum of Art, January 26–March 14, 1954, and The Museum of Modern Art, New York, April 7–June 6, 1954, catalogued page 100.

7

Edouard Vuillard 1868–1940

8 STILL LIFE WITH ONIONS AND KNIFE

Oil on canvas, $8\frac{3}{4} \times 10\frac{5}{8}$

(1890–91)

Signed upper right, "Vuillard"

Maurice Raynal sums up Vuillard's art, quoting a line from Verlaine, as one of "precise indecision." He continues: "Vuillard's 'Intimism' found an outlet in the pursuit of simplification; he stripped his work of all but essentials, using bold, highly expressive yet sober and invariably constructive lines. His feeling for precision, which was to make him the most accomplished of the 'Nabis' group, was coming into evidence. The element of 'indecision' in his work is indicated in the stylization of his tones. He uses a very thin pigment, the tones are firmly indicated but without emphasis; they are essentially variations on neutral tints, and are painted 'flat'; on whites and browns especially, recalling monastic tonalities, the garb of Dominican or Benedictine friars. On the occasions when he indulges in bright hues he mutes these, as it were, giving them deep sonorities far more emotive than his friend's rather excessive use of the 'pedal.' In fact his work brings to our mind a murmurous, spell-binding chamber music; all the more compelling for its serene restraint. If ever there was art for professionals, it is Vuillard's; and few are the artists who have not been fascinated by it."[1]

And André Gide, writing in 1905 about Vuillard's paintings: "I don't know quite what is the most admirable thing about them. Perhaps it is M. Vuillard himself. He is the most personal, the most intimate of story-tellers. I know few pictures which bring the observer so directly into conversation with the artist. I think it must be because his brush never breaks free of the emotion which guides it; the outer world, for Vuillard, is always a pretext, an adjustable means of expression. And above all it's because M. Vuillard speaks almost in a whisper – as is only right, when confidences are being exchanged – and we have to bend over towards him to hear what he says.

"There is nothing sentimental or high-falutin' about the discreet melancholy which pervades his work. Its dress is that of everyday. It is tender, and caressing; and if it were not for the mastery that already marks it, I should call it timid. For all his success, I can sense in Vuillard the charm of anxiety and doubt . . . He never strives for brilliant effect; harmony of tone is his continual preoccupation; science and intuition play a double role in the disposition of his colors, and each one of them casts new light on its neighbour, and as it were exacts a confession from it."[2]

[1] Maurice Raynal, *History of Modern Painting from Baudelaire to Bonnard,* Geneva 1949, page 96. [2] André Gide, *Gazette des Beaux-Arts,* December 1905 as quoted in the catalogue of the Roussel, Bonnard, Vuillard Exhibition, Marlborough Fine Art Ltd., London 1954, page 13.

Collection: Jacques Roussel (nephew of the artist), Paris; Sam Salz, New York.

Exhibited: Vuillard, Kunsthalle, Berne, June 22 – July 28, 1946, number 20.

8

Edouard Vuillard 1868-1940

9 WOMAN IN AN INTERIOR (Vuillard's Mother)

Oil on board, $12\frac{1}{2} \times 7$

(1891–92)

Signed lower right, "E. Vuillard"

"Mallarmé, speaking of the Parnassians, the academic poets of his time, said that they 'take the thing just as it is and put it before us – and consequently they are deficient in mystery: they deprive the mind of the delicious joy of believing that it is creating. To name an object is to do away with the three quarters of the enjoyment of the poem which is derived from the satisfaction of guessing little by little: to suggest it, to evoke it – that is what charms the imagination'.

"Vuillard was very familiar with these ideas of Mallarmé . . .

Collection: Joseph Hessel, Paris; C. S. Wadsworth Trust, New York.

"The secret charm of so many of Vuillard's small panels of the '90s is the result of his never quite 'naming' an object, as Mallarmé puts it. He 'suggests' it, he 'evokes' it, by knitting it into an amazingly complex tapestry. And by a process of telescoping planes in a picture, . . . the foreground, middleground and background overlap and fuse into a pulsating space that bears a kind of relation to the fusion of imagery in a poem by Mallarmé." (Ritchie, *Vuillard*, pages 14–16.)

Reference: Notable Paintings and Works of Art, Property of the C. S. Wadsworth Trust, New York, December 11, 1948, number 80, reproduced in the catalogue page 73.

10 GIRL AT WINDOW

Oil on board, $14\frac{1}{4} \times 10\frac{1}{4}$

(1899)

Signed lower left, "E. Vuillard"

Collection: Vuillard Family, Paris; Sam Salz, New York.

9

10

Edouard Vuillard 1868-1940

11 SELF-PORTRAIT, LE CANOTIER

Oil on canvas, 14 × 11

(1892)

Signed lower right, "E. Vuillard"

This self-portrait is, in a sense, a *pendant to* Vuillard's portrait of Toulouse-Lautrec in the museum at Albi. Not only the size but the composition and palette are so similar that they must have been painted at about the same time.

". . . the very compactness of these pictures, their smallness, packed to the edges as they are with suggestive imagery, recall Mallarmé's compressed, highly concentrated short poems. Above all, there is a Mallarméan narcissism in Vuillard's constant preoccupation not only with himself in his self portraits, but, by extension, with his mother – reading, preparing meals, at work as a dressmaker, engaging in all the endless little activities of a bourgeois housewife. It is as if he sees in her and in the beloved furnishings and patterned walls of his home a constant reminder, a projection of his whole being. This is the mystery, this is the secret of Vuillard, as narcissism in varying degrees is the secret of all his fellow symbolists." (Ritchie, *Vuillard,* pages 16, 18.)

Collection: Jacques Roussel (nephew of the artist), Paris; Sam Salz, New York.

Exhibited: Vuillard, The Cleveland Museum of Art, January 26–March 14, 1954, and The Museum of Modern Art, New York, April 7–June 6, 1954, reproduced in the catalogue page 40 as "Self Portrait in a Straw Hat".

Reference: "Self-Portraits", *Vogue,* January 1, 1958, reproduced in color, page 99.

11

Edouard Vuillard 1868-1940

12 MA GRAND'MERE

Oil on canvas, 12 × 12¼

(1894)

Signed lower left, "E. Vuillard"

Vuillard's "paintings remind me of the obverse of a tapestry; the weight of the human figure, and the gold and silver of light, and the velvet of shadow – all appear in different guise. His is an art, too, of attitudes, and folded arms, and pale hands. Vuillard has found a new and delicious way of expressing the poetry of a quiet hearth and the beauty of thought and action that underlies all poetry."[1]

"These small paintings dramatize simple people who live simple lives in an atmosphere of tranquility centered around home life. True, among the sitters are dynamic writers, thinkers, and artists, but the attitudes in which Vuillard has chosen to perpetuate them are those of relaxation."[2]

[1] Gustave Geffroy, October 29, 1893, as quoted in the catalogue of the Roussel, Bonnard, Vuillard Exhibition, Marlborough Fine Art Ltd., London 1954, page 10.
[2] Germain Seligman, in introduction to the catalogue of the Vuillard Exhibition, Jacques Seligmann & Co., New York 1948.

Collection: Jacques Roussel (nephew of the artist), Paris; Sam Salz, New York.

12

Edouard Vuillard 1868-1940

13 LA FAMILLE VUILLARD AU DEJEUNER

Oil on canvas, 12½ × 18

(1896)

Signed lower right, "E. Vuillard"

The figures around the table, left to right, are Vuillard's grandmother (compare number 12 in this catalogue, and the *Portrait of the Artist's Grandmother*, almost the same portrait in profile, which is reproduced in the Cleveland Museum and The Museum of Modern Art, New York exhibition catalogue, 1954, page 52), Vuillard's sister and wife of Roussel, and Vuillard's mother.

". . . in 1896 or 1897 when Matisse began to notice their" (Bonnard's and Vuillard's) "work at Vollard's and Durand-Ruel's he seems not to have been much impressed, or even to have struck up any special friendship with them. Yet, in spite of Matisse's retarded and sequestered experience, the three had a good deal in common. All were realists, in the broadest sense of the word. They made paintings of what they saw in the world around them, in the studio, in rooms where people lived. In his paintings of interiors Matisse had come quite close to Vuillard's intimate scenes with a woman sewing or dusting or clearing a table."[1]

"The tempo is an easy one, underlined here and there by the gathering around the supper table or the kerosene lamp of the study. Electricity is not yet in use and the telephone, with its accompanying trepidations, is unknown. There are no conflicts represented here, and if a closer approach into the minds of the sitters might reveal the struggles and anguish of life, none appears outwardly in the attitudes of the placid subjects who pursue their tasks with quiet deliberation."[2]

[1] Barr, *Matisse*, page 36. [2] Germain Seligman in introduction to the Vuillard Exhibition, Jacques Seligmann & Co., New York 1948.

Collection: Thadée Natanson, Paris; Denise Mellot, Paris; Sam Salz, New York.

Exhibited: New York Private Collections, The Museum of Modern Art, New York, June 26–September 12, 1951; *Vuillard*, The Cleveland Museum of Art, January 26–March 14, 1954, and The Museum of Modern Art, New York, April 7–June 6, 1954, reproduced page 43 in color; *Paintings from Private Collections*, The Museum of Modern Art, New York, May 31–September 5, 1955, page 21.

References: Matisse: His Art and His Public, by Alfred H. Barr, Jr., New York 1951, page 36, footnote 2 (page 530 of the Notes): "Matisse's *Dinner Table* of 1897, page 299" (formerly in the Edward G. Robinson collection and now in the Niarchos collection) "does in fact closely resemble in subject and composition Vuillard's *Vuillard Family at Lunch* of 1896 now in the collection of Mr. and Mrs. Ralph F. Colin, New York. Vuillard's design in this picture is more sophisticated with its patterning of light and dark and greater awareness of the shapes of voids and solids; and so is his rather mannered drawing."; "Modern Shows Choices of Five Collectors", by Belle Krasne, *The Art Digest*, August 1, 1951, reproduced page 17; "Rockefeller, Whitney, Senior, Odets, Colin", by Henry McBride, *Art News*, Summer 1951, page 36.

13

Edouard Vuillard 1868-1940

14 PORTRAIT OF THE PAINTER ROUSSEL

Oil on board, $25\frac{1}{2} \times 17$

1898

Signed lower right, "E. Vuillard 98"

"Vuillard's immediate school friends were Ker-Xavier Roussel, who was to marry his sister; Maurice Denis, whose interest in art profoundly influenced him, and Lugné-Poë, who was to become one of the most dynamic actor-managers of the Paris theatre of the '90s and who came to serve as an enthusiastic liaison between the writer and painter symbolists of his day.

"Roussel, whom he met in 1884, was Vuillard's closest friend and it was he who seems to have influenced him most and got him to study at the Ecole des Beaux Arts, beginning in 1886, where Gérôme conducted one of the master classes. Growing discontented with the school and the teaching there, they joined forces in 1888 with a group of young rebel students at the Académie Julian, where Bouguereau was the chief teacher. This group, which included Maurice Denis, Sérusier, Bonnard, Ibels, Piot, Séguin, Valloton and Ranson, banded together and early in 1889 called themselves the Nabis, a name derived from the Hebrew word for prophet."[1]

"At the Galerie Bernheim there is a painter, M. Roussel, who is gentle but determined, a dreamer and a man of meditation, bent on bringing to us, through harmonies of colour, the meaning and the poetry of the world around him. He achieves his object; beneath his appearance of softness and timidity there lies a concealed strength."[2]

[1] Ritchie, *Vuillard*, page 9. [2] Gustave Geffroy, *La Vie Artistique*, Paris, July 9, 1899, as quoted in the catalogue of the Roussel, Bonnard, Vuillard Exhibition, Marlborough Fine Art Ltd., London, page 11.

Collection: Gaston Bernheim de Villers, Paris, from the artist; Sam Salz, New York.

Exhibited: Galerie Bernheim-Jeune, Paris 1907; *Vuillard Exhibition*, Galerie Bernheim-Jeune, Paris, February 1938; *Vuillard*, The Cleveland Museum of Art, January 26–March 14, 1954, and The Museum of Modern Art, New York, April 17–June 6, 1954, reproduced in the catalogue page 77.

References: Vuillard, by André Chastel, *Art News Annual 1954*, reproduced page 49; *Vuillard*, by Curt Schweicher, Bern 1955, plate 18.

E Vuillard 98

Edouard Vuillard 1868-1940

15 SYMPHONIE EN ROUGE

Oil on board, 23 × 25¾

(1899-1900)

Signed lower right, "Vuillard"

Vuillard's "mother, a native of Paris, and twenty-seven years younger than her husband, decided on his death to occupy herself and support her family by going into business as a dressmaker. Her love and knowledge of the materials of her craft, which she was to transmit to her artist son, she must have come by directly. Her father and brother were both textile designers."[1]

"Having explored to his complete satisfaction the extreme possibilities of the redness of red, the greenness of green, the blueness of blue, and having 'assembled' his colors in a striking variety of orders, retaining to the full the flatness of his panel or canvas, he proceeded to explore as early as 1893, in what one feels is in a Mallarméan spirit, the mysterious possibilities of an infinite gradation of color hues to extract thereby the subtlest overtones, the essential perfume of intimate objects and activities in and about his home."[2]

[1] Ritchie, *Vuillard*, page 8. [2] *ibid*, page 13.

Collection: Bernheim-Jeune, Paris; Bignou Gallery, New York.

Exhibited: L'Art Français Contemporain, Palais de la France, New York World's Fair, Summer 1939, number 160, reproduced in the catalogue; *A 20th Century Selection*, Bignou Gallery, New York, March 4–29, 1947, number 14 as "Interior with Figure"; *Works of Art Belonging to Alumnae*, Smith College Museum of Art, Northampton, Massachusetts, May–June 1950, number 36; *New York Private Collections*, The Museum of Modern Art, New York, June 26 – September 12, 1951; *Collector's Choice*, Paul Rosenberg & Co., New York, March 17–April 18, 1953, number 6, reproduced in the catalogue page 25; *Vuillard*, The Cleveland Museum of Art, January 26–March 14, 1954, and The Museum of Modern Art, New York, April 17–June 6, 1954, where it is dated 1893, reproduced in the catalogue page 28 in color.

References: Art News, March 1953, reproduced on the cover in color; *Vuillard*, by André Chastel, *Art News Annual 1954*, reproduced page 42 in color; "E. Vuillard", *Life*, November 1, 1954, reproduced page 76 in color, and dated 1893.

15

Henri Matisse 1869-1954

16 GUITARISTE

Oil on canvas, 21½ × 15

(1903)

Signed lower right, "Henri Matisse"

Referring to Matisse's "Dark Period" between 1901 and 1904, Alfred H. Barr, Jr., writes: "Except for innumerable *académies* or classroom drawings. . . his copies in the Louvre, and the rather incidental characters in his interiors. . . Matisse had done no figure painting during the first ten years of his career. His finished compositions had been predominantly still lifes. . . Now, during his dark period, he gained sufficient confidence to send several landscapes, heads and figure paintings to the Indépendants. Indeed his most important canvases of the period are figures.[1]

". . . Matisse has not much lightened his palette in the *Guitarist*. . . a small canvas of his wife costumed as a Spanish guitar player, but the painting is altogether livelier than the severe *Carmelina* or the dour *La coiffure*. The staccato contrasts of light and shade, the glitter of the costume so deftly distinguished from the flowered hanging, contribute to an effect quite unlike anything Matisse had achieved before, an effect which looks forward prophetically to the vivacious Rococo of his paintings of the early 1920s. But there are other values in the *Guitarist* which the pleasant pictures of twenty years later do not have, a beauty of surface for instance and a certain intensity of feeling conveyed partly by the dramatic lighting, partly by the active tension of the figure's unstable swastika pose."[2]

"The bright face of the guitar, slanting across the figure, creates depth and continuity of depth. And the entire composition revolves around the exactly centered black hole, which also acts, rather abruptly and ambiguously, to lock the plane of the figure to that of the dark gap between curtain and wall on the right."[1]

[1] Barr, *Matisse*, page 49. [2] *ibid*, page 51. [3] Clement Greenberg, *Henri Matisse*, New York 1953, facing plate 10.

Collections: Bernheim-Jeune, Paris; Baron Edouard von der Heydt, Ascona; Alfred Daber, Paris; Sam Salz, New York.

Exhibited: Matisse Exhibition, Galeries Georges Petit, Paris 1926; *Works of Art Belonging to Alumnae*, Smith College Museum of Art, Northampton, Massachusetts, May–June 1950, number 59; *The Eye Listens – Music in the Visual Arts*, Dwight Art Memorial, Mount Holyoke College, South Hadley, Massachusetts, October 23–November 15, 1950, number 70; *Henri Matisse*, The Museum of Modern Art, New York, November 13, 1951–January 13, 1952, number 9, reproduced in the catalogue page 15. Also shown The Cleveland Museum of Art, February 5–March 16, 1952, The Art Institute of Chicago, April 1–May 4, 1952, The San Francisco Museum of Art, May 22–July 6, 1952, Los Angeles Municipal Art Department, July 24–August 17, 1952; *Paintings from Private Collections*, The Museum of Modern Art, New York, May 31–September 5, 1955, catalogued page 14; *Exposition Retrospective Henri Matisse*, Musée National d'Art Moderne, Paris, July 28–November 18, 1956, number 10; *Les Fauves*, Dallas Museum for Contemporary Arts, January 29–March 16, 1959, number 26.

References: Matisse, by Roland Schacht, Dresden 1922, reproduced page 57; *Henri Matisse*, by Elie Faure and others, Paris 1923, plate 2; *Matisse: His Art and His Public*, by Alfred H. Barr, Jr., New York 1951, pages 41, 43, 45, 51 and 53, reproduced page 310; "Matisse at his Best", by Thomas B. Hess, *Art News*, December 1951, page 40; *Saturday Review*, January 5, 1952, page 35; "Matisse Answers Twenty Questions", *Look*, August 23, 1953, reproduced page 72 in color; *Henri Matisse*, by Clement Greenberg, New York 1953, reproduced in color, plate 10; *Henri Matisse*, by Gaston Diehl, Paris 1954, referred to page 27 as "Guitariste assise" and dated 1904; *Henri Matisse*, by Sam Hunter, The Metropolitan Museum of Art Miniatures, New York 1956, plate 2; *Matisse*, by Jacques Lassaigne, Geneva 1959, page 59.

Henri Matisse

Henri Matisse 1869-1954

17 LA GANDOURA VERTE (The Green Gandoura Robe)

Oil on wood panel, 12⅞ × 9⅜

(1916)

Signed upper left, "Henri Matisse"

This monumental miniature, with its brilliant green and mauve, is one of a series of portraits of the model Lorette painted by Matisse in 1916–17, called by Barr "perhaps the greatest" (years) "of Matisse's career as a painter."[1] Over these two years "a broad movement is evident, a movement from austerity of structure, line, color and sentiment toward a more relaxed and decorative art."[2]

Yet despite this movement, it is true, as Henry Clifford has written that: "Through all the years and all the periods the same Matisse persists, civilized, cerebral, intellectual and always French. He is abandon with order, license with restraint. While his apparent simplicity is disarming, in reality, his frank straight line contains the complexity of a maze. Matisse is indeed a challenge to us all. It is easy enough to enjoy his simple surface pattern and go no deeper; but those who use his line, as Ariadne's thread, can reach the heart of the labyrinth where they will find his ultimate truth."[3]

[1] Barr, *Matisse*, page 181. [2] *ibid*, page 189. [3] Catalogue of Henri Matisse Reprospective Exhibition, Philadelphia Museum of Art 1948, page 11.

Collection: Frederic C. Bartlett, Jr., Manchester, Vermont; Pierre Matisse, New York.

Exhibited: Henri Matisse, Pierre Matisse Gallery, New York, January 23–February 24, 1934, number 23; *Henri Matisse, Retrospective Exhibition of Paintings, Drawings and Sculpture,* Philadelphia Museum of Art, April 1 – May 9, 1948, number 40, reproduced in the catalogue; *Some Paintings from Alumnae Collections,* Smith College Museum of Art, Northampton, Massachusetts, June 1948; *New York Private Collections,* The Museum of Modern Art, New York, June 26–September 12, 1951; *Exposition Retrospective Henri Matisse,* Musée National d'Art Moderne, Paris, July 28–November 18, 1956, number 45.

Reference: Henri Matisse, by Gaston Diehl, Paris 1954, page 69 as "La robe gandoura verte".

17

Henri Matisse 1869-1954

18 JEUNE FILLE EN VERT A LA FENETRE (Girl in Green)

Oil on canvas, $25\frac{1}{2} \times 21\frac{1}{2}$

(1921)

Signed lower left, "Henri Matisse"

"Matisse moved to the French Riviera in 1917 and the world changed. Gone was the austerity and restraint – gone forever was any attempt at geometric cubism or rigid linearism. To understand this period one must have known and loved any Mediterranean shore; the relaxed atmosphere – the intense light diffused through the scented leaves of eucalyptus trees, the brilliance of the earth, the dark tree trunks, the perfume of mimosa. And all this against the amethyst blue of the unruffled Mediterranean . . . Matisse had always loved the richness of eastern colors, the Opulence of Turkish carpets, of Persian miniatures and of Coptic stuffs. . . ."[1]

"His paintings of the years 1920–25 appear to be perfect expressions of a serene, industrious and uneventful life. . . Girls looking out of the window or playing the piano or violin in the apartment at Nice, or girls costumed as odalisques in oriental pantaloons and embroidered jackets, or nude, standing before patterned textiles or tiled screens, lolling on rug-strewn divans; still lifes of fruit and flowers, richly furnished interiors in which a dozen different colors, textures and patterned surfaces are magically harmonized in a hedonistic, sensual and charming art with no challenging or difficult moments – except for the painter."[2]

"The *Girl in Green* in the Ralph F. Colin collection, New York, was painted in the apartment on the Place Charles-Félix and is more indicative of Matisse's direction in 1921 than either the big grey *Interior* done earlier in the year or the *Woman before an Aquarium*. Again flowers and figures are balanced in a delicate equilibrium, enriched by arabesques, bright striplings and the blue sea seen through the shutters – decorative elements which appear again and again in pictures of this and the following year. Many of them however lack the relatively firm and thoughtful structure of the *Girl in Green* . . . "[3]

[1] Henry Clifford in catalogue of the Matisse Retrospective Exhibition, Philadelphia Museum of Art, 1948, page 10.
[2] Barr, *Matisse*, page 198. [3] *ibid*, page 210.

Collection: Galerie Druet, Paris; Marcel Kapferer, Paris; Etienne Bignou, Paris; Valentine Gallery, New York; Lillie P. Bliss, New York; Museum of Modern Art, New York.

Exhibited: Exposition de Collectionneurs au profit de la Société des Amis du Luxembourg, Paris, March–April 1924, number 120; *Memorial Exhibition, The Collection of the Late Miss Lillie P. Bliss*, The Museum of Modern Art, New York, May 17–September 27, 1931, number 94, reproduced in the catalogue; *The Collection of Miss Lillie P. Bliss*, Fourth Loan Exhibition, Addison Gallery of American Art, Andover, Massachusetts, October 17–December 15, 1931, number 72; *Modern Masters from the Collection of Miss Lillie P. Bliss*, John Herron Art Institute, Indianapolis, January 1–31, 1932, number 68, reproduced in the catalogue; *Lillie P. Bliss Collection*, The Museum of Modern Art, New York, 1934, number 45, reproduced in the catalogue; *Les Maîtres de l'Art Indépendant, 1895–1937*, Petit Palais, Paris, June–October 1937, number 5 as "Femme à la fenêtre (1922)"; *Exhibition of Modern French Painting*, Skidmore College, Saratoga Springs, New York, February 8–25, 1942, number 21 as "Young Girl in Green"; *New York Private Collections*, The Museum of Modern Art, New York, June 26–September 12, 1951; *19th Century Influences in French Painting*, Guild Hall, East Hampton, New York, August 14–September 8, 1952, number 25; *Exposition Retrospective Henri Matisse*, Musée National d'Art Moderne, Paris, July 28–November 18, 1956, number 60 and plate XXVI as "Jeune Fille en vert à la Fenêtre".

References: Matisse, by Henry McBride, New York 1930, reproduced number 35 as "La dame en vert (à la fenêtre)"; *The Arts*, January 1930, reproduced page 339; "Henri Matisse", *Les Chroniques du Jour*, April 1931, plate 15; *International Studio*, June 1931, reproduced page 41; *Henri Matisse*, by Christian Zervos and others, Paris and New York 1931, reproduced facing page 72 as "Interior, Nice 1920"; *Expressionism in Art*, by Seldon Cheney, New York 1934, reproduced page 265; *Henri Matisse*, by Pierre Courthion, Paris 1934, as "Jeune fille en mauresque robe verte"; *Matisse*, by R. Kawashima, Tokyo 1936, reproduced in color; *Henri Matisse*, by Raymond Escholier, Paris 1937, reproduced facing page 72 as "Femme accoudée

18

References (continued):

à sa fenêtre"; *Coronet,* July 1938, reproduced page 13 in color; *Notable Paintings and Sculpture . . . Property of The Museum of Modern Art,* New York, May 11, 1944, number 83, reproduced in the catalogue page 49; "Is there Chaos in Art?" by Sam A. Lewisohn, *The New York Times Magazine,* March 4, 1945, page 19; *Styles in Painting,* by Paul Zucker, New York 1950, reproduced page 257, figure 208; *Matisse: His Art and His Public,* by Alfred H. Barr, Jr., New York 1951, page 210; "Rockefeller, Whitney, Senior, Odets, Colin", by Henry McBride, *Art News,* Summer 1951, reproduced page 36; "Gallery Notes, Preview of 1960", by Dorothy Gees Seckler, *Art in America,* Number Four 1959, reproduced in color page 101.

Henri Matisse 1869-1954

19 ODALISQUES

Oil on canvas, $21\frac{1}{2} \times 29\frac{1}{2}$

1928

Signed lower right, "Henri Matisse 1928"

Although many, including Dr. Barnes, "who has analyzed Matisse's paintings more thoroughly than any other critic,"[1] feel that the period 1920 to 1925 is the most attractive and satisfactory in Matisse's entire career, Barr concludes: "Whether or not Matisse consciously intended to challenge some of his greatest paintings of a decade or two before, and whether or not he succeeded, it is clear that the adventurous, experimental spirit of 1926–28 produced the most memorable paintings of the decade. . . . The figure – more often there are two – the floor, the wallpaper, even the Venetian mirror on the wall are all present but a formidable Baroque has been reduced to a charming Rococo, sharper in color, more vigorous in drawing, crisper in detail, more compact in composition than the Rococo of 1920–25 but essentially the same in spirit. Matisse had again lowered his sights to a more comfortable range."[2]

[1] Barr, *Matisse*, page 208. [2] *ibid*, page 215.

Collection: Valentine Gallery, New York; Stephen C. Clark, New York.

Exhibited: Henri Matisse, Galerie George Petit, Paris, June 16–July 25, 1931, number 135 as "La Partie de Dames"; *Henri Matisse, Retrospective Exhibition of Paintings, Drawings and Sculpture*, Philadelphia Museum of Art, April 1–May 9, 1948, number 72, reproduced in the catalogue; *Some Paintings from Alumnae Collections*, Smith College Museum of Art, Southampton, Massachusetts, June 1948; *Henri Matisse*, Paul Rosenberg & Co., New York, April 5–May 1, 1954, number 13, reproduced in the catalogue.

References: The Arts, January 1930, reproduced page 342; "How to Frame and Hang your Pictures", by Van Day Truex, *House & Garden*, December 1940, reproduced page 130; *Henri Matisse*, by Gaston Diehl, Paris 1954, page 82 as "Odalisques jouant aux dames"; *Matisse*, by Jacques Lassaigne, Geneva 1959, reproduced page 102 in color as "Two Odalisques Playing Checkers".

19

Henri Matisse 1869-1954

20 RECLINING FIGURE

Pencil on paper, 16 × 20½

1941

Signed lower right, "Henri Matisse '41"

"The still lifes, interiors and figures of 1941 and 1942, even more than usual, are but the visible top of a great iceberg of effort. Beneath them, supporting them, though comparatively tentative, obscure and private, lie score upon score of drawings. Matisse was always drawing, but now the quantity and quality of his work in crayon and ink made an impression even upon himself (who was ordinarily so dissatisfied). From Nice, on April 3, 1942, he wrote Pierre in New York: 'For a year now I've been making an enormous effort in drawing. I say *effort*, but that's a mistake, because what has occurred is a *floraison* after fifty years of effort. . . '." (Barr, *Matisse*, page 268.)

Collection: Curt Valentin Gallery, New York.

Exhibited: Drawings by Contemporary Painters and Sculptors, Curt Valentin Gallery, New York, December 16, 1952–January 10, 1953, number 59; *The Sculpture of Henri Matisse,* Curt Valentin Gallery, New York, February 10–28, 1953, number 44.

21 RESTING MODEL

Ink on paper, 16 × 20

1946

Signed lower left, "Matisse 46"

Collection: Curt Valentin Gallery, New York.

22 HEAD OF A GIRL

Ink on paper, 15¾ × 10¼

1947

Signed lower left, "H. Matisse Mai '47"

Collection: Curt Valentin Gallery, New York.

Exhibited: The Sculpture of Henri Matisse, Curt Valentin Gallery, New York, February 10–28, 1953, number 54.

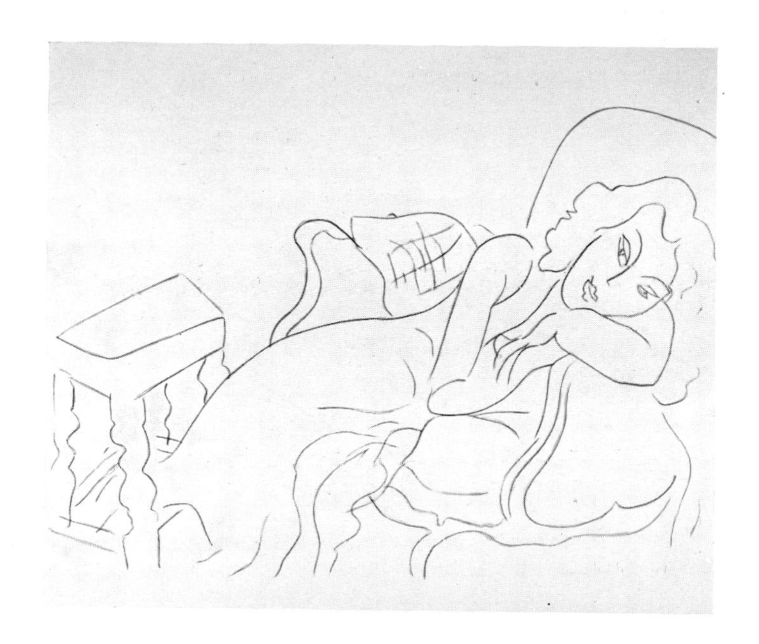

20

21

22

Lyonel Feininger 1871-1956

23 YELLOW VILLAGE CHURCH III

Oil on canvas, $31\frac{1}{2} \times 39\frac{1}{2}$

1937

Signed upper right, "Feininger 1937"; *signed on the stretcher,* "Lyonel Feininger 1937 'Village Church' "

"Actually, Feininger's art was as unique in Germany as the artist himself seemed at the Bauhaus. Against the *Sturm und Drang* of German expressionism with its heavy pigment and violent color, against the later abstractionists and dadaists and the hard-boiled satirical realism of the *Neue Sachlichkeit*, Feininger's subject matter and his refinement both of structure and feeling stand out in marked contrast. Equally apart from German art stood two other foreigners, both colleagues of Feininger's at the Bauhaus, the Russian, Kandinsky, and the half-French Swiss, Paul Klee.

"To find a close parallel to Feininger among authentically German painters one must go back a hundred years to Caspar David Friedrich, the great romantic painter of Gothic ruins and Baltic horizons. Of modern German artists only Franz Marc bears some resemblance. Both Marc and Feininger learned much from the French cubists and both retained a strong romantic feeling. Marc in his animal paintings, Feininger in his sea vistas and Gothic towns. Marc, however, before his death in 1916 had already passed into a style of brightly colored, decorative abstraction which has not stood the test of time. Feininger's work by contrast has grown less abstract in the past twenty-five years. Instead of running into the impasse of flat two-dimensional abstraction, as did the French cubists of 1920, he has used cubist line and plane to enhance as well as to assimilate pictorially the shapes of ships and buildings in the deep spaces of sky and sea." (Alfred H. Barr, Jr., in the catalogue to the exhibition of *Feininger-Hartley*, The Museum of Modern Art, New York 1944, page 11.)

Collection: Julia Feininger (widow of the artist).

Exhibited: Lyonel Feininger, Mrs. Cornelius J. Sullivan Gallery, New York, November 7–26, 1938, number 8; *Exhibition of Contemporary American Painting*, California Palace of the Legion of Honor, San Francisco, May 17–June 17, 1945, reproduced in the catalogue; *Lyonel Feininger*, (*80th Birthday Exhibition*) Curt Valentin Gallery, New York, March 18–April 12, 1952, number 12, reproduced in the catalogue; *Lyonel Feininger*, Bayerische Akademie der schönen Künste, Munich, September 3–October 10, 1954 and Kestner-Gesellschaft, Hanover, October 17–November 21, 1954, number 18, reproduced in the catalogue; *Lyonel Feininger*, Stedelijk Museum, Amsterdam, December 10, 1954–January 17, 1955, number 18, reproduced in the catalogue; *Lyonel Feininger Memorial Exhibition*, San Francisco Museum of Art, November 5–December 13, 1959, number 50. This exhibition was, and will be, shown at Minneapolis Institute of Arts, January 5–February 7, 1960, Cleveland Museum of Art, February 18–March 20, 1960, Albright Art Gallery, Buffalo, April 8–May 8, 1960, Museum of Fine Arts, Boston, May 19–June 26, 1960.

Reference: Lyonel Feininger, by Hans Hess, Stuttgart 1959, mentioned page 136 as "Gelbe Dorfkirche III", catalogued and reproduced page 284, number 382.

Not included in the exhibition at The Knoedler Gallery, April–May 1960.

23

Lyonel Feininger 1871-1956

24 PARIS: SEINE AT NIGHT

Watercolor on paper, 12 × 18½

1951

Signed lower left, "Feininger" *and dated lower right* "15.10.51"

" 'What I want to do is to capture some of the cosmic wonders.' These words of Lyonel Feininger in a letter to me seem to sum up what I feel about his work, that he does just this, for in his art I am conscious of drift of cloud and movement of sea as color moves to embrace color, or tears forth to exist in its own intensity setting up contrapuntal rhythms which challenge the eye in an exciting manner . . .

". . . Feininger's domain is the great Universal Nature herself which surrounds us all. Year by year he seeks to penetrate deeper and deeper into his mysterious realm. He captures all her moods. The aftermath of storm – of golden sun, and the cool light of autumnal skies. In his paintings the sea and sky, the lower and upper world interlock in embrace, clouds hover over their reflections, and old ruins rise on hills and speak to us of time and decay . . .

"Recognition of the known is in all his paintings but never realism. He does not abstract for abstraction's sake. He draws the essence from the real, reshapes and relates in color, form and line – and gives us his world wherein, if we have the willing mind, and take the time, we are rewarded by becoming more aware, and more sensitive within ourselves." (Mark Tobey in catalogue of *Feininger Exhibition* at Curt Valentin Gallery, New York, 1954).

Collection: Julia Feininger (widow of the artist).

Exhibited: Lyonel Feininger, Willard Gallery, New York, March 6–April 12, 1958, number 20; *Sixth Annual Exhibition,* Museum of Art of Ogunquit, Maine, June 28–September 8, 1958, number 22; *Lyonel Feininger, Paintings of Harbors, Ships and the Sea,* Busch-Reisinger Museum, Harvard University, October 6–November 8, 1958, page 8 of the catalogue.

25 SUNSET WITH BLUE AREA

Watercolor on paper, 11¾ × 18½

1953

Signed lower left, "Feininger 1953"

Collection: Julia Feininger (widow of the artist).

Exhibited: Lyonel Feininger, Willard Gallery, New York, March 6–April 12, 1958, number 23; *Sixth Annual Exhibition,* Museum of Art of Ogunquit, Maine, June 28–September 8, 1958, number 25; *Lyonel Feininger, Paintings of Harbors, Ships, and the Sea,* Busch-Reisinger Museum, Harvard University, October 6–November 8, 1958, page 8 of the catalogue.

24

25

Georges Rouault 1871-1958

26 HEAD OF A WORKMAN (Head of Christ?)

Oil on paper, $15\frac{1}{2} \times 11\frac{1}{4}$

1911

Signed upper left, "G. Rouault 1911"

"From 1905 to 1918 Rouault produced the magnificent paintings of prostitutes, clowns, judges and Christs which have earned him rank as one of the major artists of our century."[1]

"Rouault. . . really is not a portrait painter, and the distinction between him and Soutine in this respect is worth making. Soutine dwells on the personalities of his lowly men and women; he dramatizes their oddity and their loneliness; he thinks of them as important but misunderstood. Whereas Rouault is thinking not of people but of humankind, with a general compassion, a feeling of equal universal guilt, and according to this thought he creates a mask, a set of masks. His imagination is based upon the Christian faith, which is a great leveller or equalizer."[2]

[1] James Thrall Soby, *Contemporary Painters*, New York 1948, page 96. [2] Monroe Wheeler, *20th Century Portraits*, New York 1942, page 16.

Collection: J. B. Neumann, New York; Pierre Matisse, New York.

Exhibited: Georges Rouault: Paintings and Prints, The Museum of Modern Art, New York, April 3–June 3, 1945, number 27, reproduced in the catalogue page 56, in the 2nd edition of the catalogue, number 27, reproduced page 60; *Works of Art Belonging to Alumnae*, Smith College Museum of Art, Northampton, Massachusetts, May–June 1950, number 72; *New York Private Collections*, The Museum of Modern Art, New York, June 26–September 12, 1951; *Mostra di Georges Rouault*, Galleria d'Arte Moderna, Padiglione d'Arte Contemporanea, Milan, April–June 1954, number 25 as "Testa d'Operaio".

References: Georges Rouault, by Lionello Venturi, New York 1940, plate 43 as "Tête d'ouvrier", 2nd edition Paris 1948, plate 41; *Twentieth Century Painters*, by Bernard Dorival, New York 1958, volume 1, page 38 as "Workman's Head, 1911".

26

Georges Rouault 1871-1958

27 THE BLUE ANGEL

Gouache, oil and pastel on paper, $17\frac{1}{2} \times 10\frac{1}{2}$

(1912)

Signed upper right, "G. Rouault"

Variously known as *Young Girl* and *The Blue Girl*, the title of *The Blue Angel* has finally been chosen because of the intensely religious medievalism which it emanates. Its painting manner is modern but its directness, simplicity and emotional appeal are eternal and ageless. In earlier references the painting has been dated 1912, but it may well have been painted up to five years later; for it differs greatly from the tortured works of Rouault's early period.

"The two periods, early and middle, show profound differences of approach. By 1916 Rouault's spiritual crisis of 1905–06 has abated somewhat. The artist's grief is still unassuaged, but his emotion is muted and controlled by a mature dignity; to vicious protest has succeeded a resignation which surrenders nothing of pity but much of hate. And this change in spirit is reflected in his increased interest in painterly methods. . .

". . . The slashing, nervous overwriting and the massed shadows of the earlier period have disappeared. Indeed, in occasional works of the war years, modeling is achieved almost entirely through gradation of soft tone, and line is merely accentual in function. The color is no longer handled as an atmospheric wash of dark and limited range, but is built up through repeated applications which give it a luminous quality. The tones are melded rather than contrasted, as they were ten years before. The key is more brilliant and by 1917 included rose, bright yellow and pink in addition to the red, green, blue, white, brown, chrome and black of his earlier career." (Soby, *Rouault*, pages 19–20.)

Collection: Dikran G. Kelekian, New York; Lee A. Ault, New York; Valentine Gallery, New York.

Exhibited: Georges Rouault Retrospective Loan Exhibition, The Institute of Contemporary Art, Boston, The Phillips Memorial Gallery, Washington, The San Francisco Museum of Art, November 1940–March 1941, number 66 as "Young Girl", reproduced in the catalogue; *Paintings and Prints by Georges Rouault*, The Renaissance Society at the University of Chicago, October 5–31, 1945, number 5 as "The Blue Girl".

References: "The Full Stature of Rouault", by Alfred M. Frankfurter, *The Art News*, November 9, 1940, page 8; "How to Frame and Hang your Pictures", by Van Day Truex, *House & Garden*, December 1946, reproduced page 130.

27

Georges Rouault 1871-1958

28 THE JUDGE

Oil on paper, $26\frac{1}{4} \times 20\frac{1}{2}$

(1927)

Signed lower left, "G. Rouault"

"Around 1907 Rouault began several satirical paintings of judges whom he presents, in a critic's apt phrase, as 'between the bear and the ass.' Judges were for him, as they had been for Daumier, symbols of bourgeois corruption, of justice become a travesty of itself through the callousness of the prosperous middle classes."[1] The work is rare, if not unique, in that Rouault presents this Judge as a jolly soul whose red nose indicates his love of wine and the glint in whose eyes testifies to a probably equal attachment to women and song. The traditional date of the painting, 1927, may be misleading. It was probably started much earlier.

"Rouault, as we know, has often worked on the same canvas over a period of five, ten or even twenty years, sometimes retouching it almost steadily, sometimes holding it in wait for the final enrichment of a day's elation or a year's distress. He has painted thinly in wash; he has piled layer on layer of pigment; he has used an unconventional technique of oil, watercolor, pastel and crayon, in unpredictable combinations."[2]

[1] Soby, *Rouault*, page 17. [2] James Thrall Soby, *Contemporary Painters*, New York 1948, pages 96–7.

Collection: Valentine Gallery, New York; Lee A. Ault, New York; Pierre Matisse, New York.

Exhibited: Georges Rouault Retrospective Loan Exhibition, The Institute of Contemporary Art, Boston, The Phillips Gallery, Washington, The San Francisco Museum of Art, November 1940–March 1941, number 44, reproduced in the catalogue; *French Paintings*, Pierre Matisse Gallery, New York, October 1941, number 16; *Paintings and Prints by Georges Rouault*, The Renaissance Society at the University of Chicago, October 5–31, 1945, number 8; *School of Paris*, Valentine Gallery, New York, March 25–April 13, 1946, number 19 as "Juge" and dated 1932; *Some Paintings from Alumnae Collections*, Smith College Museum of Art, Northampton, Massachusetts, June 1948; *New York Private Collections*, The Museum of Modern Art, New York, June 26–September 12, 1951; *Mostra di Georges Rouault*, Galleria d'Arte Moderna, Padiglione d'Arte Contemporanea, Milan, April–June 1954, number 34 as "Il giudice", plate XXI; *Paintings from Smith Alumnae Collections*, Smith College Museum of Art, Northampton, Massachusetts, October 14–November 18, 1959, number 25, reproduced in the catalogue page 63.

Reference: "School of Paris", by Margaret Bruening, *The Arts Digest*, April 1, 1946, page 18.

28

Georges Rouault 1871-1958

29 BOUQUET

Oil on paper, 35 × 23¾

(1938)

Signed lower left, "G. Rouault"

From 1916 to 1929, Rouault devoted himself largely to print making. "When Rouault began again to paint steadily, around 1929, his art almost immediately reflected a widening of inspirational source . . . It seems likely, too, that his literary studies were combined with a more extensive research into the art of the past than he had undertaken before. . . His paintings of 1929–39 indicate an appreciation of Byzantine enamels, Roman mosaics and Coptic tapestries. . ." Many of them "are so heavily painted as to justify a critic's description of certain Rouaults as 'rotten with color'.

"Considering his still lifes and figure pieces of 1939–46, it seems possible that Rouault predicted wrongly when, in praising Renoir for very opposite attainments, he described himself as 'prisoner of shadows until my death'." (Soby, *Rouault*, pages 25–28.)

Collection: Valentine Gallery, New York.

Exhibited: Georges Rouault: Paintings and Prints, The Museum of Modern Art, New York, April 3–June 3, 1945, number 77, reproduced page 89. In the 2nd edition of the catalogue, 1947, number 77, reproduced page 97 in color; *Summer Loan Show,* The Metropolitan Museum of Art, July–August 1950; *New York Private Collections,* The Museum of Modern Art, New York, June 26–September 12, 1951; *Rouault Retrospective Exhibition,* The Cleveland Museum of Art, January 27–March 15, 1953, The Museum of Modern Art, New York, March 31–May 31, 1953, catalogued page 29, Los Angeles County Museum, July 3–August 16, 1953, catalogued page 31; *Mostra di Georges Rouault,* Galleria d'Arte Moderna, Padiglione d'Arte Contemporanea, Milan, April–June 1954, number 49 as "Mazzo di Fiori".

References: Georges Rouault, by Lionello Venturi, New York 1940, plate 147 as "Le Vase de fleurs", 2nd edition, Paris 1948, plate 153; *Georges Rouault,* by Jacques Maritain, New York 1952, reproduced page 21 in color; "Rouault: Great Mystic Paints Good Friday but never Easter", by Wintrop Sargeant, *Life,* February 2, 1953, reproduced page 61 in color; *Georges Rouault,* by Jacques Maritain, New York 1954, plate 35 in color.

Georges Rouault 1871-1958

30 MILLE ET UNE NUIT

Oil on canvas, 10 × 15¼

(1939)

Signed lower right, "G. Rouault"

"This period of regained serenity" (the late '30s) "might also be described as a period of concentration on pictorial technique rather than on imagery. So it was only natural for Rouault's interest in landscape (already noted in his work of the twenties) to continue unabated and even increase. He probably found, as others had before him, that landscape is less engrossing than the human figure and thus allows greater license to the creative imagination.

"After 1932 he invented a new type of landscape, which had only been hinted at in his earlier work. These new landscapes are visions of the East, seen in the light of the setting sun and peopled with figures amongst whom we often discern that of Christ . . . They might be described as Rouault's sacred landscapes.

". . . Figures and objects are roughly sketched in, dimly visible through a swirling harmony of gorgeous colors. Figures make no gestures: they are presented, not represented, with the result that the whole dramatic effect of the work springs from the colors and the desolation of the scene. That desolation recurs in all Rouault's landscapes. For him, apparently, the earth was a wasteland; even the houses are dismal; their occupants wander among them as among so many ruins. Christ and a few paupers represent humanity amid this desolation. Life and light are only to be sought above, in the heavens. This is an apocalyptic vision of nature, its bleakness redeemed only by the thirst for color and light, by the sustaining aspiration toward a Kingdom not of the world. Dedicated to the setting sun, these landscapes contain some of Rouault's loveliest visions of color." (Lionello Venturi, *Rouault*, Paris 1959, pages 105–106.)

Collection: Pierre Matisse, New York.

30

Georges Rouault 1871–1958

31 GIRL WITH TURBAN

Oil on panel, 13 × 9½

(1940?)

Unsigned

"In . . . other recent pictures Rouault has turned to a new lyricism of color which reaches perhaps its purest form in still life subjects. The rage of his early period (1903–06) has abated almost entirely; the melancholy of his middle years (1915–18) has lifted so that even a relatively tragic subject like *The Wounded Clown* is treated fairly dispassionately, and depends for its impact upon more traditional esthetic qualities which survive to an exceptional degree the picture's translation into tapestry . . .

" 'Glory to you', he adds in speaking of Renoir, 'for often having been drunk with color when so many others sought only a mediocre success and withered away.' He himself . . . showed signs of that resurgence of spirit, expressed through color, which carried Renoir into his strong later period . . . a statement by him . . . confirms the more serene direction his art is taking: 'I spent my life painting twilights. I ought to have the right now to paint the dawn'." (Soby, *Rouault*, pages 27–28.)

Collection: Ambroise Vollard, Paris; M. Knoedler & Company, Inc., New York.

31

Clayton S. Price 1874-1950

32 ABSTRACTION IV

Oil on board, $25\frac{1}{2} \times 29\frac{1}{2}$

(1944)

Signed lower right, "C. S. Price"

"Unlike the typical 'Western' paintings, Price's works are charged with feeling. In the 'Western' all details must be 'correct' and nothing essential to the story may be omitted. It says to the spectator, 'Here are the facts; make up your own mind.' The artist is a reporter, remaining neutral as to any emotional implications . . .

"In the paintings of Price's mature period, there are no details, only essences. They say, 'Here is the spirit of the thing and the way I feel about it. Look long, and it will move you, too.' Feeling is the thing, not the fact but feeling, deep in the soul of mankind: love, fear, humility, patience, grief, joy, devotion, and other nameless emotions which only the right combination of subject and form can evoke." (Harris K. Prior in the Price Memorial Exhibition, Portland, Oregon, 1951, page 17.)

Collection: Valentine Gallery, New York.

Exhibited: First New York Exhibition of Paintings by C. S. Price, Valentine Gallery, New York, March 12–31, 1945, number 17; *Works of Art Belonging to Alumnae*, Smith College Museum of Art, Northampton, Massachusetts, May–June 1950, number 70; *C. S. Price Memorial Exhibition*, Portland Art Museum, Portland, Oregon, March 8–April 18, 1951, number 68, reproduced in the catalogue page 49. Also shown at Seattle Art Museum; Los Angeles County Museum; Baltimore Museum of Art; Munson–William–Proctor Institute, Utica, New York; Detroit Institute of Art; Walker Art Center, Minneapolis; California Palace of the Legion of Honor, San Francisco; Santa Barbara Museum of Art; *C. S. Price*, The Downtown Gallery, New York, January 28 – February 21, 1958, number 12.

Reference: "Margaret Bruening Writes", *Arts*, February 1958, page 51.

32

Gwen John 1876-1939

33 PORTRAIT STUDY OF WINIFRED JOHN

Pencil on paper, $6\frac{1}{4} \times 6\frac{1}{4}$

(1910–12)

Signed lower left, "Gwen John"

"In tenderness and intensity of spirit, Gwen John may be compared with her contemporary in letters, Katherine Mansfield. The sister of Augustus, she was retiring, while he is flamboyant; she painted on a small scale with great deliberation and infinite delicacy, while he exhausts himself quickly in brilliant improvisations.

"Her life was spent in self-imposed obscurity, mostly in France. She studied at the Slade School, then went to Whistler's short-lived school in Paris. She was a devoted admirer of Whistler and later formed an intimate friendship with Rodin . . . She was deeply religious and in later life joined the Catholic Church. In many respects, in fact, she was like a nun all her life, a nun in retreat, with painting her outlet for spiritual contemplation and expression. Her art, with all its delicacy and femininity, has power and conviction and it is surely this mysterious mixture of grace and strength that makes it so arresting. She seldom exhibited during her lifetime and it is only since her death that her work has begun to be fully appreciated." (Andrew Carnduff Ritchie in *Masters of British Painting 1800–1950*, The Museum of Modern Art, New York 1956, page 104.)

Collection: Edwin John (nephew of the artist, son of her sister, the sitter); Matthiesen Ltd., London.

33

Paul Klee 1879-1940

34 FRAUEN PAVILLON (Women's Pavilion)

Oil on board, $15\frac{3}{4} \times 20\frac{1}{8}$

1921

Signed upper right "Klee" *and on reverse* "1921/121 Klee Frauen Pavillon"

Klee . . . . "has been accused of being a 'literary' painter. For the person who still insists on regarding painting as decorative, or as surface texture, or pure, formal composition the accusation is just. But Klee defies the purists and insists, as do Chirico and Picasso, upon the right of the painter to excite the imagination and to consider dreams as well as still life material for their art. . . .

"Nothing is more astonishing to the student of Klee than his extraordinary variety. Not even Picasso approaches him in sheer inventiveness. In quality of imagination also he can hold his own with Picasso; but Picasso of course is incomparably more powerful. Picasso's pictures often roar or stamp or pound; Klee's whisper a soliloquy – lyric, intimate, incalculably sensitive." (Alfred H. Barr, Jr., in Introduction to *Paul Klee*, The Museum of Modern Art, New York, pages 6–7.)

Collection: Hugo Stinnes, Essen; Gunther Francke, Munich; Kleeman Galleries, New York.

Exhibited: Works of Art Belonging to Alumnae, Smith College Museum of Art, Northampton, Massachusetts, May–June 1950, number 54; *Summer Loan Show*, The Metropolitan Museum of Art, New York, July–August 1950; *Paintings by Paul Klee 1879–1940*, Society of the 4 Arts, Palm Beach, March 9–April 1, 1951, number 16; *New York Private Collections*, The Museum of Modern Art, New York, June 26–September 12, 1951, number 23; described by Emily Genauer in *New York Herald Tribune* review of the exhibition, Sunday, July 1, 1951: ". . . has a luminosity of surface and solidity of form rare in the work of this Swiss surrealist"; *L'Oeuvre du XXe Siècle*, Musée National d'Art Moderne, Paris, May–June 1952, number 46; *XXth Century Masterpieces*, The Tate Gallery, London, July 15–August 17, 1952, number 41.

References: Deutsche Malerei der Gegenwart, by Fritz Nemitz, Munich 1948, reproduced in color facing page 40; *Paul Klee*, by Will Grohmann, New York n.d., catalogued page 143, number 161, reproduced in color page 163, mentioned pages 245 and 246.

34

Paul Klee 1879-1940

35 PORTAL EINER MOSCHEE (Portal of a Mosque)

Watercolor on paper, $14\frac{3}{4} \times 11\frac{1}{2}$

1931

Signed upper left "Klee" *and below* "1931 S 1 Portal einer Moschee"

"In an age that blasted privacy Paul Klee built a small but exquisite shrine to intimacy.

"Klee did not belong to the tradition of the great decorators. Though he derived from the German expressionist school that stemmed out of van Gogh and Munch, he was a designer in feathers rather than in flame. In an age that felt 'it was necessary to shake an adult to get a reaction out of him', Klee lived fully in elaborating nuances and in capturing fancies. He was not a painter whose work speaks to us from a distance. Klee was fundamentally a cabinet artist who should be read and re-read, in a manner of speaking, on the knee. The subtle complexity of his texture justifies it. He spoke in a mixed tongue of representational and technical phantasy. These were fused by a remarkably untrammeled sensibility. The result was a curious pictorial poetry all its own. And in this character of so much of Klee's work we often feel a closer affinity with Oriental art than with that of the Occident." (James Johnson Sweeney, "The Place of Paul Klee," in *Paul Klee*, The Museum of Modern Art, New York, 1945, page 18.)

Collection: Curt Valentin Gallery, New York.

Reference: Paul Klee, by Will Grohmann, New York n.d., catalogued page 418, number 311, reproduced in the classified catalogue, number 87, mentioned page 213.

Paul Klee 1879-1940

36 DRAWING "150"

Ink on paper, 7½ × 5½

1914

Unsigned but dated at the bottom "1914 150"

"Perhaps one day among twentieth-century art's many distinctions will be counted the rediscovery of visual wit as a relatively independent species of humor. The sculptors of the Middle Ages who created gargoyles as a relief from the tensions of faith, occasional draftsmen of the Renaissance and the Baroque, tribal craftsmen averting their own heady fears, the Daumier who noted Louis Philippe's resemblance to a pear – these and innumerable other artists through the ages understood that humor can be a matter of visual notation purely. But many more artists have been illustrators of a humor which either stemmed from verbal descriptions or could be conveyed equally well in words. We think at once of the Dutch and Flemish masters for whom drinking, vomitting and urination were so appealing a theme; of the later satirists who borrowed from the theatre such comic personages as The Ailing Female, The Miser and The Hypochondriac; of the genre painters of the nineteenth century, so tiresomely devoted to homely long-winded anecdotes. In our own century, however, a few important artists have brought humor again within the fairly separate range of plastic expression, and among these Klee, Miro and Calder are outstanding." (James Thrall Soby, *Contemporary Painters*, New York 1948, page 99.)

Collection: Curt Valentin Gallery, New York.

Exhibited: Paul Klee – Sixty-six Unknown Drawings, Curt Valentin Gallery, New York, April 11–23, 1955, number 1.

37 KINDERBILDNIS (Child's Portrait)

Ink on paper, 13 × 5¼

1923

Signed lower left "23 Klee 3/12" *and below* "1923 229"

Collection: Curt Valentin Gallery, New York.

Exhibited: Klee – Sixty Unknown Drawings, Buchholz Gallery, New York, January 16–February 3, 1951, number 23; *Paul Klee Drawings 1908–1940*, The Museum of Modern Art, New York, Circulating Exhibition, 1953/1954; *Fifty Drawings by Paul Klee (Collection of Curt Valentin, New York)*, Institute of Contemporary Arts, London, November 18–December 31, 1953, number 19; *Paul Klee – Max Beckmann*, Kestner-Gesellschaft, Hanover, January 17–February 24, 1954, number 19; *Paul Klee Handzeichnungen*, Galerie Schüler, Berlin, March 16–April 14, 1954, number 19.

References: Paul Klee, Handzeichnungen II, 1921–1930, by Will Grohmann, Berlin 1934, catalogued page 21, number 60, plate 16; *The Drawings of Paul Klee*, by Will Grohmann, New York 1944, plate 16.

36

37

Paul Klee 1879-1940

38 ELISE

Ink on paper, $11\frac{1}{2} \times 6\frac{7}{16}$

1926

Signed upper left "Klee" *and below* "1926 W 6 Elise"

"If all three artists" (Klee, Miro, Calder) "are among modern art's finest humorists – and they are, of course, much more than that – there are important differences in the quality of their wit. Of the three, only Klee was mystic in the intensity of his laughter. In a previous book on Klee's prints, I referred to his 'spirituality of humor,' and I can now find no other term to describe the etherial nature of his perception. It is true that many of his pictures are based on specific incidents or observed natural phenomena, so that he never lost contact with reality altogether. But his vision was transcendental, and he achieved in the end an almost religious profundity of humor. Deeply musical, he seemed to translate optical sensation into another language, communicating with the very core of our consciousness. He was assuredly the greatest, incomparably the most varied, visual humorist of our time, and his own brilliant accomplishment is described in a quotation from Gogol which Klee included in his diary for 1904: 'There is a laughter which is to be put on the same dignified level as higher lyrical emotions, and which is as distant as heaven from the convulsions of a vulgar clown'." (James Thrall Soby, *Contemporary Painters*, New York 1948, page 103.)

Collection: Curt Valentin Gallery, New York.

Exhibited: Paul Klee – Sixty-six Unknown Drawings, Curt Valentin Gallery, New York, April 11–23, 1955, number 27.

Reference: Paul Klee, Handzeichnungen II, 1921–1930, by Will Grohmann, Berlin 1934, catalogued page 27, number 129.

Klee
1926 W 6
Elise

Paul Klee 1879-1940

39 DIE ALTE (Old Woman)

Pencil on paper, 13¾ × 9¾

1926

Signed lower center "Klee" *and below* "1926 G1 die Alte"

"Klee's drawings provide a key to his art as a whole . . . All of Klee's works spring from deep sources. No other living artist is so aware of Goethe's perception that man cannot long remain conscious without plunging into the unconscious, where lies the root of his existence, for the conscious and the subconscious are strong factors in his work. In this Klee is no exception; we can observe such tendencies in his contemporaries, in artists like Picasso, in writers like Joyce, and in musicians like Hindemith." (Will Grohmann, *The Drawings of Paul Klee*, New York 1944, pages i and ii.)

Collection: Curt Valentin Gallery, New York.

Exhibited: Klee – Sixty Unknown Drawings, Buchholz Gallery, New York, January 16–February 3, 1951, number 32; *Paul Klee Drawings 1908–1940,* The Museum of Modern Art, New York, Circulating Exhibition, 1953/1954; *Fifty Drawings by Paul Klee (Collection of Curt Valentin, New York),* Institute of Contemporary Arts, London, November 18–December 31, 1953, number 26, reproduced in the catalogue; *Paul Klee – Max Beckmann,* Kestner-Gesellschaft, Hanover, January 17–February 24, 1954, number 26; *Paul Klee Handzeichnungen,* Galerie Schüler, Berlin, March 16–April 14, 1954, number 26.

Reference: Paul Klee, Handzeichnungen 1921–1930 by Will Grohmann, Berlin 1934, catalogued page 26, number 83. (Compare another version of the same subject in crayon, reproduced plate 33 in *The Drawings of Paul Klee*, by Will Grohmann, New York 1944.)

40 AELTLICHES KIND II (Oldish Child)

Carbon rubbing on paper, 19 × 12¾

1930

Signed lower center "Klee" *and below* "1930 B 2 ältliches Kind II"

Collection: Curt Valentin Gallery, New York.

Exhibited: Klee – Sixty Unknown Drawings, Buchholz Gallery, New York, January 16–February 3, 1951, number 44, reproduced in error as number 46; *Paul Klee Drawings 1908–1940,* The Museum of Modern Art, New York, Circulating Exhibition, 1953/1954; *Fifty Drawings by Paul Klee (Collection of Curt Valentin, New York),* Institute of Contemporary Arts, London, November 18–December 31 1953, number 36; *Paul Klee – Max Beckmann,* Kestner-Gesellschaft, Hanover, January 17–February 24, 1954, number 36; *Paul Klee Handzeichnungen,* Galerie Schüler, Berlin, March 16–April 14, 1954, number 36.

Reference: Paul Klee, Handzeichnungen 1921–1930, by Will Grohmann, Berlin 1934, catalogued page 37, number 79.

39

40

Fernand Léger 1881–1955

41 LES TROIS PERSONNAGES DEVANT LE JARDIN

Oil on canvas, $25\frac{1}{2} \times 36$

1922

Signed lower right, "F. Leger 22"

"With majestic restraint Léger now [1920] embarks on a series of paintings devoted to men and women, but these figures are so impersonally handled, so classically devoid of emotion as to be almost denials of the human body. Rousseau's influence can be detected in *The Mechanic* where the magnified form (almost like a close-up from motion pictures, a field in which Léger is soon to experiment) recalls the bluntness and humor of folk art, while *Three Women*[1] follows more in the established tradition of Poussin, father of French classicism and a painter greatly admired by Léger. The astute organization of this canvas, where every circle, rectangle and line functions for the entire composition, demonstrates how imperiously the artist transforms human anatomy at will. The painting is constructed like a heavy monument in which stylized hair, breasts, and hands contribute to the whole. Though the figures themselves do not move, the forms within the canvas carry the observer's eye back and forth, up and down, by means of echoing repetitions and connecting lines and forms."[2]

"For me the human figure, the human body, has no more importance than keys or bicycles. It's true. These are for me objects of plastic value to be used as I wish.

"A painter should not try to reproduce a beautiful thing, but should make the painting itself a beautiful thing."[3]

[1] The reference is to *Le Grand Déjeuner* in the collection of The Museum of Modern Art, New York, Mrs. Simon Guggenheim Fund, the culmination of the series of which the painting catalogued was a part. [2] Katherine Kuh, *Léger: A Survey of his Art*, in catalogue of Léger exhibition, The Art Institute of Chicago 1953, page 30. [3] Statements by Léger, *ibid*, page 31.

Collection: Georges Bernheim Gallery, Paris; Mrs. Eliane Oppenheimer, Paris, New York; Niveau Gallery, New York.

Exhibited: Some Paintings from Alumnae Collections, Smith College Museum of Art, Northampton, Massachusetts, June 1948; *Fine Art from Private Collections*, Staten Island Museum, January 11–February 12, 1958, number 22.

Reference: The New York Times, Sunday, January 12, 1958, reproduced page 79.

41

Fernand Léger 1881–1955

42 COMPOSITION IN BLACK AND YELLOW

Oil on canvas, 36 × 29

1942

Signed lower right, "42 F. Leger"

"In 1940 Léger embarked on his fourth visit to America where he remained until after the war, returning to France in 1946. From these years came some of his greatest paintings. The enormous vitality of the United States challenged him so intensely that, despite his typically Gallic background, he became one of America's most astute interpreters. By recognizing that the new world does not and need not resemble Europe he discovered its indigenous beauty, commenting that 'there is poetry in the machine age in America' . . .

"These . . . paintings . . . come from three summers Léger spent at Rouses Point in New York, where he used an abandoned farm as the basis for his work . . ." (The) "pictures show how impressed he was by the American phenomenon of waste and growth . . ."[1]

"I prefer to see America through its contrasts – its vitality, its litter and its waste. Perhaps this is because I am most responsive to externals. Perhaps it is my old interest in the object.

"Near Lake Champlain where I spent the summers of 1943, 1944 and 1945, I was even more struck by the broken down farm-machines I would come across abandoned in the fields. For me it became a typical feature of the American landscape, this carelessness and waste and blind and ruthless disregard of anything worn or aged.

"I painted a group of American landscapes, being inspired by the contrast presented by an abandoned machine – become old scrap iron – and the vegetation which devours it."[2]

[1] Katherine Kuh, *Léger: A Survey of his Art,* in catalogue of Léger exhibition, The Art Institute of Chicago, 1953, pages 54 and 60. [2] Statements by Léger, *ibid,* page 61.

Collection: Valentine Gallery, New York, from the artist.

42
F.LEGER

Pablo Picasso 1881-

43 VASE DE FLEURS

Oil on canvas, $36\frac{1}{2} \times 28\frac{1}{2}$

(1907)

Signed lower left, "Picasso"

"Sympathy for the violent expression and primitive strength of negro sculpture came at a moment when Picasso was again preoccupied with the realisation of solid forms on a two-dimensional surface. His thoughts were inspired by sculpture, but it was not until two years later that he turned his hand again to modelling. Before this happened, though he thought as a sculptor, he acted as a painter. Even in a still-life such as *Flowers on a Table*, the flowers are endowed with such solidarity as to suggest the possibility of making a reconstruction in bronze. The planes, luminous with colour, are determined by strong outlines and heavy shading, a technique which suggests the fronds of a palm or the tattooed patterns on the naked bodies of negro statues. . . .

"These influences were assimilated and combined with the persistent love that Picasso had for archaic Iberian bronzes. . . . To label all paintings of this period as 'Negro' is in fact to oversimplify the problem of their origins and diminish their significance. Raynal suggests that it would be less misleading to call this period 'prehistoric' or 'pre-hellenistic', but if the period must have a label it would be more exact to use the term 'proto-cubist' invented by Barr, since all these tendencies led consistently to the birth of the new style." (Roland Penrose, *Picasso: His Life and His Work*, London, 1958, page 132).

Collection: Purchased from the Artist in 1910 by Wilhelm Uhde, Berlin and Paris; Paul Edward Flechtheim, Paris (Flechtheim Gallery, Berlin); Mrs. Yvonne Zervos, Paris; Pierre Loeb, Paris; Mrs. Meric Callery, New York; Galerie Pierre, Paris.

Exhibited: Picasso, Thannhauser Galleries, Berlin, February 1913, number 30 as "Stilleben mit schwarzem Kamin und Kaktus, 1907"; *Summer Loan Show*, Metropolitan Museum of Art, New York, July–August 1950; *New York Private Collections*, The Museum of Modern Art, New York, June 26–September 12, 1951; *Picasso 75th Anniversary Exhibition*, The Museum of Modern Art, New York, May 20 – September 8, 1957 and The Art Institute of Chicago, October 29–December 8, 1957, catalogued and reproduced page 34; *Picasso, A Loan Exhibition of his Paintings, Drawings, Sculpture, Ceramics, Prints and Illustrated Books*, The Philadelphia Museum of Art, January 8–February 15, 1958, number 42, reproduced in the catalogue.

References: Picasso, by Maurice Raynal, Munich 1921, plate 29; *Pablo Picasso*, by Christian Zervos, Paris 1942, Volume II, "Oeuvres de 1906 à 1912", part 1, page 17, plate 30 as "Fleurs sur une Table" and dated "Summer 1907"; *Notable Modern French and other Paintings . . .*, New York, January 17 and 18, 1945, number 57, reproduced in the catalogue, page 27; *Picasso*, by Jaime Sabartés, Paris and New York 1946, plate 3 in color as "Flowers"; *Picasso* by Maurice Raynal, Geneva 1953, reproduced in color page 43; *Picasso*, by Frank Elgar and Robert Maillard, Paris 1955, reproduced (no pagination); *Picasso: His Life and Work*, by Roland Penrose, London 1958, referred to page 132 as "Flowers on a Table".

Pablo Picasso 1881-

44 TETE CUBISTE

Oil on canvas, $14\frac{1}{2} \times 12\frac{1}{2}$

(1910)

Signed lower left, "Picasso"

"The two years from his completion of the *Demoiselles d'Avignon* late in the spring of 1907 to his departure for Horta de Ebro early in the summer of 1909 were for Picasso a time of exploration in which there was much trial and perhaps some error.

"At Horta Picasso's style seemed suddenly to crystallize, literally and visually as well as metaphorically. The new style, or better, method has been called 'analytical cubism'. Analytical cubism developed for several years and then changed gradually into 'synthetic' cubism, the watershed between the two occurring about 1912. Like most terms applied to the visual arts, 'analytical' is not very exact yet it does describe in a general way the cubist process of taking apart or breaking down the forms of nature. 'Analytical' also conveys something of the spirit of investigation and dissection of form carried on by Picasso and Braque almost as if their studios were laboratories. Not that their analyses were scientific or mathematical. In spite of its 'geometrical' style and certain analogies to space-time physics, cubism, like all painting worthy of the name of art, was a matter primarily of sensibility, not science." (Barr, *Picasso*, page 66.)

Collection: Perls Galleries, New York; Walter P. Chrysler, Jr., New York.

Exhibited: Collection of Walter P. Chrysler, Jr., Virginia Museum of Fine Arts, Richmond, January 16–March 4, 1941, number 164, and Philadelphia Museum of Art, March 28–May 11, 1941; *Classic and Romantic Traditions in Abstract Painting*, Circulating Exhibition of the Museum of Modern Art, New York, 1939–40.

References: Pablo Picasso, by Christian Zervos, Paris 1942, Volume II, "Oeuvres de 1906 à 1912", part 1, page 80, plate 162 as "Têtes, Horta de Ebro, Summer 1909" where it is the left-hand portion of a larger (longer) canvas. A note states that the painting was cut in two after it left the studio of Picasso and the resulting canvases were relined; *French and Other Modern Paintings, Drawings, Prints from the Collection of Walter P. Chrysler, Jr.*, New York, March 22, 1945, number 79, reproduced in the catalogue page 49; "Oeuvres et Images Inédits de la jeunesse de Picasso" by Christian Zervos, *Cahiers d'Art*, Volume 25, Number II, 1950, reproduced in a photograph of Picasso's studio at Horta de Ebro, page 279 (the complete canvas before cutting).

44

Pablo Picasso 1881-

45 LA TABLE DE TOILETTE

Oil on canvas, 24 × 18¼

(1910)

Signed upper left, "Picasso", *and also on back of canvas*

"Cubism is no different from any other school of painting. The same principles and the same elements are common to all. The fact that for a long time cubism has not been understood and that even today there are people who cannot see anything in it, means nothing. I do not read English, an English book is a blank book to me. This does not mean that the English language does not exist, and why should I blame anybody else but myself if I cannot understand what I know nothing about?" (Statement by Picasso, 1923, in Barr, *Picasso*, page 270.)

Collection: Ambroise Vollard, Paris; Galerie Pierre, Paris; Walter P. Chrysler, Jr., New York; Valentine Gallery, New York.

Exhibited: Picasso, Primera Exposición en Madrid organizada por ADLAN, (Amigos de las Artes Nuevas) 1936, number 3; *Picasso Exhibition,* Valentine Gallery, New York, October 26–November 21, 1936; *Selected Works from the Walter P. Chrysler, Jr. Collection,* The Arts Club, Chicago, January 1937, number 37; *Selected Exhibition of the Walter P. Chrysler, Jr. Collection,* Detroit Institute of Arts, October 1937, number 5 as "Chez L'Artiste – La Table de Toilette – Abstraction"; *Classic and Romantic Traditions in Abstract Painting,* Circulating Exhibition of the Museum of Modern Art, New York, 1939–40; *Collection of Walter P. Chrysler, Jr.,* The Virginia Museum of Fine Arts, January 16–March 4, 1941, number 166 and reproduced in the catalogue, and The Philadelphia Museum of Art, March 29–May 11, 1941; *1910–1912, The Climactic Years in Cubism,* Jacques Seligmann & Company, New York, October 16–November 6, 1946, number 12; *Cubism,* Buchholz Gallery, New York, April 5–30, 1949, number 41.

References: Picasso, by Jean Cassou, Paris, London and New York 1940, reproduced page 75 as "The Dressing Table"; *Pablo Picasso,* by Christian Zervos, Paris 1942, Volume II, "Oeuvres de 1906 à 1912", part I, page 108, plate 220 and dated "Paris Spring 1910"; *Picasso,* by Joan Merli, Buenos Aires, 2nd Edition, 1948, plate 199.

45

Pablo Picasso 1881-

46 LE RAMEUR (The Rower)

Oil on canvas, 28⅜ × 23⅜

(1910)

Signed on the back of the canvas, "Picasso"

"Many think that cubism is an art of transition, an experiment which is to bring ulterior results. Those who think that way have not understood it. Cubism is not either a seed or a foetus, but an art dealing primarily with forms, and when a form is realized it is there to live its own life. A mineral substance, having geometric formation, is not made so for transitory purposes, it is to remain what it is and will always have its own form. But if we are to apply the law of evolution and transformation to art, then we have to admit that all art is transitory. On the contrary, art does not enter into these philosophic absolutisms. If cubism is an art of transition I am sure that the only thing that will come out of it is another form of cubism." (Statement by Picasso, 1923, Barr, *Picasso*, page 271.)

Collection: Ambroise Vollard, Paris; 509 Gallery, New York; Earl Horter, Philadelphia; Pierre Matisse Gallery, New York.

Exhibited: 1910–1912, The Climactic Years in Cubism, Jacques Seligmann & Company, New York, October 16–November 6, 1946, number 11; *New York Private Collections,* The Museum of Modern Art, New York, June 26–September 12, 1951; *The Struggle for New Form,* World House Galleries, New York, (Opening Exhibition) January 22–February 23, 1957, number 67; *An Inaugural Exhibition, El Greco, Rembrandt, Goya, Cézanne, Van Gogh, Picasso,* Milwaukee Art Institute, September 12–October 20, 1957, number 89, reproduced in the catalogue page 71; *Cubism in Retrospect 1911–1929,* Denver Art Museum, January 22–February 22, 1959, number 30, reproduced in the catalogue.

References: Pablo Picasso, by Christian Zervos, Paris 1942, Volume II, "Oeuvres de 1906 à 1912", part 1, page 115, plate 231 and dated "Cadaquès Summer 1910"; "Rockefeller, Whitney, Senior, Odets, Colin" by Henry McBride, *Art News,* Summer 1951, reproduced page 36.

Pablo Picasso 1881–

47 SCULPTURE NEGRE

Oil on canvas, $28\frac{5}{8} \times 19\frac{5}{8}$

1929

Signed upper left, "Picasso 29"

In 1929, Picasso was thinking of huge monuments which could be both houses for living in and enormous sculptures of women's heads, and which would be set up along the Mediterranean coast. "It is plain, then, that painting was sometimes a second best for Picasso, since material difficulties and the lack of suitable opportunities came in the way of his higher ambitions. . . . One of the attractive things about Picasso is that sometimes he made paintings while thinking in terms of sculpture, and at other times sculptures that showed a painter's hand . . . He always longed to combine the most fantastic imagination with the crudist reality, to bring together what is usually dissociated, to unite contraries, to seize on what is discontinuous in nature and cast it into the continuum of the work of art. And he never lost the sly pleasure he found in shocking, astonishing or baffling others with his endless tricks and feats." (Frank Elgar and Robert Maillard, *Picasso*, New York, 1956 pages 150 and 152.)

Collection: Wildenstein & Cie., Paris; Valentine Gallery, New York; Walter P. Chrysler, Jr., New York.

Exhibited: Exposition Umelecka Berada, Prague, 1931; *Picasso 21 Paintings – 1908 to 1934*, Valentine Gallery, New York, November 7–26, 1938, number 18; *Classic and Romantic Traditions in Abstract Painting*, Circulating Exhibition of the Museum of Modern Art, New York, 1939–40; *Collection of Walter P. Chrysler, Jr.*, The Virginia Museum of Fine Arts, January 16–March 4, 1941, number 182, reproduced in the catalogue, and The Philadelphia Museum of Art, March 29–May 11, 1941; *Works of Art Belonging to Alumnae*, Smith College Museum of Art, Northampton, Massachusetts, May–June 1950, number 68.

References: French and Other Modern Paintings, together with a Group of American Primitive Paintings from the Collection of Walter P. Chrysler, Jr., New York, April 11, 1946, number 32 as "Sculpture Negre; Femme", reproduced in the catalogue, page 23; *Picasso*, by Joan Merli, Buenos Aires, 2nd edition, 1948, plate 370 as "Escultura negra"; *Pablo Picasso*, by Christian Zervos, Paris 1955, Volume VII, "Oeuvres de 1926 à 1932", page 98, plate 247 as "Buste de Femme".

47

Pablo Picasso 1881-

48 BONNET ROUGE

Oil on canvas, $57\frac{5}{8} \times 44\frac{3}{4}$

1934

Signed lower right, "Picasso XXXIV"

"During the summer at Cannes, he [Picasso] had visited Barcelona where he went to the bull ring. In September he began the long series of more or less fantastic bull fight pictures which after many strange mutations were to culminate four years later in the *Guernica*. . . .

"The physical and psychological violence of the bullfight paintings was balanced throughout 1934 and the early months of 1935 by a score or more of paintings of girls gravely reading, writing or drawing, with demurely lowered eyes. Superficially their mood is quiet; yet the deep glowing color, the heavy drawing, and the silent concentration of the figures suggest in some of these paintings an inward intensity of feeling." (Barr, *Picasso*, pages 186 and 188.)

Collection: Mrs. Valentine Dudensing, from the artist.

Exhibited: New York Private Collections, The Museum of Modern Art, New York, June 26–September 12, 1951.

References: Picasso 1930–1935, by Christian Zervos and others, Paris, n.d., reproduced page 108 as "Peinture 1934"; *Picasso*, by Joan Merli, Buenos Aires 1948, plate 413 as "Pintura"; "Rockefeller, Whitney, Senior, Odets, Colin" by Henry McBride, *Art News*, Summer 1951, page 36; *Picasso* by Maurice Raynal, Geneva 1953, reproduced in color page 96, as "Woman in a red Hat"; *Pablo Picasso* by Christian Zervos, Paris 1957, volume VIII, "Oeuvres de 1932 à 1937", page 111, plate 241 as "Femme assise".

Pablo Picasso 1881–

49 LE COQ

Pastel on paper, $30\frac{1}{2} \times 21\frac{1}{4}$

1938

Signed lower right, "Picasso 29.3.38"

"During 1938 Picasso worked with unusual energy and richness of invention . . .

"Among his figures of 1938 *Girl with a Cock* . . . is the most shocking in subject. Through the power of Picasso's imagery what might seem perverse and minor sadism takes on the character of hieratic ritual, perhaps even a symbolic significance. . . .

"In several large drawings and pastels done a few weeks later the trussed, prone and helpless fowl in the *Girl with a Cock* revives to match the strength and pride of the eagle. While he was at work on one of the series a young American painter, Xavier Gonzales, same to see him. 'Cocks', Picasso said, 'there have always been cocks, but like everything else in life we must discover them – just as Corot discovered the morning and Renoir discovered girls . . . Cocks have always been seen, but never as well as in American weather vanes.' " (Barr, *Picasso*, pages 212 and 214.)

Collection: Perls Gallery, Paris; Walter P. Chrysler, Jr., New York; Valentine Gallery, New York.

Exhibited: Picasso – Forty Years of his Art, The Museum of Modern Art, New York, November 15, 1939–January 7, 1940, number 348 and The Art Institute of Chicago, February 1–March 3, 1940 and St. Louis Museum, March 16–April 14, 1940 and Museum of Fine Arts, Boston, April 26–May 25, 1940 and San Francisco Museum of Art, June 25–July 22, 1940; *Collection of Walter P. Chrysler, Jr.,* The Virginia Museum of Fine Arts, Richmond, January 16–March 4, 1941, number 186, reproduced in the catalogue, and The Philadelphia Museum of Art, March 29–May 11, 1941; *Some Paintings from Alumnae Collections,* Smith College Museum of Art, Northampton, Massachusetts, June 1948; *Picasso 75th Anniversary Exhibition,* The Museum of Modern Art, New York, May 20–September 8, 1957, catalogued and reproduced page 80 and The Art Institute of Chicago, October 29 – December 8, 1957; *Picasso A Loan Exhibition of His Paintings, Drawings, Sculpture, Ceramics, Prints and Illustrated Books,* The Philadelphia Museum of Art, January 8 – February 23, 1958, number 196, reproduced in the catalogue.

References: The New York Times Magazine, Sunday, November 12, 1939 reproduced page 14; *Picasso,* by Joan Merli, Buenos Aires, 2nd Edition 1948, plate 500 as "El gallo"; *Picasso,* by Maurice Raynal, Geneva 1953, reproduced in color page 103; *Graphis,* number 56, 1954, reproduced in color on cover; *Pablo Picasso,* by Christian Zervos, Paris 1958, Volume IX, "Oeuvres de 1937 à 1939", page 54, plate 113; "The Picasso Zoo", *The New York Times Magazine,* Sunday, July 5, 1959, reproduced page 31.

49

Georges Braque 1882-

50 THE TABLE

Oil on canvas, 15 × 21½

(1910)

Signed on the back of the canvas, "Braque"

". . . there was a crucial period in Picasso's career – namely the heroic years of Cubism (1909–14) – when he became so deeply involved in creative activity with a great French artist, Georges Braque, that for a while he virtually shared his personality. And as a result of this 'marriage' [to quote Picasso's own expression] between the French and Spanish temperaments, not only was the whole course of modern art vitally changed but indeed the French tradition has been [and is still being] enriched and a succession of masterpieces have been added to our artistic heritage. Cubism was the joint creation of Braque and Picasso working on equal terms, and during the period of its elaboration we must beware of trying to differentiate between their respective contributions or to weigh up the relative importance of the one against the other. Suffice it to say that whereas Picasso's cubist works tend to be more sculptural, more emphatically linear and more direct in their appeal, Braque's are perhaps more painterly, more lyrical, more exquisite and more serene. Admittedly, at the time – and indeed until 1919 – most people thought of Braque (who is by nature modest and retiring) as a follower of Picasso. But with all the evidence at our disposal nowadays we know that there is no truth in this view. We can see Cubism nascent in Braque's work before it occurs in that of Picasso . . ." (Douglas Cooper, "Georges Braque: the Evolution of a Vision", in catalogue of the Braque Exhibition, The Royal Scottish Academy, Edinburgh, August 18–September 15, 1956, and The Tate Gallery, London, September 28–November 11, 1956, page 5.)

Collection: Daniel Henry Kahnweiler, Paris; Alfred Flechtheim, Berlin; Mme. Mendelssohn-Bartholdi, London; Mayor Gallery, London; Buchholz Gallery, New York; Walter P. Chrysler, Jr., New York; Scott & Fowles, New York.

Exhibited: Braque Retrospective Exhibition, The Arts Club, Chicago, November 1939, number 42 and Phillips Memorial Gallery, Washington, December 6, 1939–January 6, 1940, number 16 and San Francisco Museum of Art, February 1940, number 42; *Collection of Walter P. Chrysler, Jr.,* The Virginia Museum of Fine Arts, Richmond, January 16–March 4, 1941, and The Philadelphia Museum of Art, March 29–May 11, 1941, number 20; *Works of Art Belonging to Alumnae,* Smith College Museum of Art, Northampton, Massachusetts, May–June 1950, number 41; *Summer Loan Show,* Metropolitan Museum of Art, New York, July–August 1950; *New York Private Collections,* The Museum of Modern Art, New York, June 26–September 12, 1951, number 20; *Cubism 1910–1912,* Sidney Janis Gallery, New York, January 3–February 4, 1956, number 3, reproduced in the catalogue.

Reference: "Georges Braque" by George Isarlov, *Orbes,* Spring 1932, catalogued page 83, number 101 as "L'eventail, 38 × 55 cm. – (K 1012)" and dated 1911.

50

Georges Braque 1882-

51 CERET: THE ROOFTOPS

Oil on canvas, 32⅜ × 23¼

(1911)

Signed on the back of canvas, "Braque"

"The sculptor Manolo, a friend of Picasso's, lived at Céret, a small town on the French side of the Pyrenees and at his suggestion several of the group decided to spend the summer of 1911 there. This produced such a flourishing of new painting that Maurice Raynal later called Céret the 'Barbizon of Cubism'. Picasso and Fernande, among the first to arrive, had rented a house. Braque and Marcelle Lapré found an apartment nearby. The paintings of both artists now developed such a shallow depth that the volumes, instead of receding, gave the illusion of rising like relief sculpture away from a background that remained close to the surface of the canvas. Because of its crowded, shut-off space this was sometimes called 'hermetic cubism'."[1]

"The present picture, a townscape seen through an open window [details such as chimneys and sloping roof can be discerned], . . . Note the diagonal composition rising triangularly up the canvas, which is more characteristic of Braque than of Picasso.

"Braque painted two or three other views of Céret at this time, his last landscapes until 1928–9. One of these [coll. Müller, Solothurn] is very similar to the present composition and perhaps served as a preparatory study."[2]

[1] Henry R. Hope, *Georges Braque,* New York, 1949, page 53. [2] Douglas Cooper, catalogue of *Braque Exhibition,* The Royal Scottish Academy, Edinburgh, August 18–September 15, 1956, and the Tate Gallery, London, September 28–November 11, 1956, page 33, notes to number 27.

Collection: Daniel Henry Kahnweiler, Paris; Baron Robert von Hirsch, Basel; Perls Gallery, New York.

Exhibited: Cubism 1910–1912, Sidney Janis Gallery, January 3–February 4, 1956, number 4 as "Les Toits de Paris", reproduced in the catalogue; *G. Braque,* The Royal Scottish Academy, Edinburgh, August 18–September 15, 1956, and The Tate Gallery, London, September 28–November 11, 1956, number 27, plate 14a.

References: "Georges Braque", by George Isarlov, *Orbes,* Spring 1932, catalogued page 83, number 116 as "La Fenêtre (Céret, Pyrénneés-Orientales) *81 × 64 cm.* – (K 1022)"; *Cubism,* by Guy Habasque, Geneva 1959, reproduced in color page 53, as "The Rooftops".

51

13694

Maurice Utrillo 1883-1955

52 LES TOITS A SARCELLES (Rooftops at Sarcelles)

Oil on board, 21 × 28½

(1909)

Signed lower left, "Maurice Utrillo"

"Although Maurice Utrillo (born 1883) painted a few promising pictures before and some attractive pictures after his best period, it is becoming more and more certain that only during the brief span of the years 1909 to 1914 was there enough personal expression and painterly distinction in his work to justify his reputation as a master in the great tradition of French painting. Then it was that he revealed himself as a rare combination of 'popular painter' and 'painters' painter', an unthinking artisan and yet an outstanding technician who somehow achieved sentient effects of texture and exquisite relations of color which the most accomplished brushmen have envied . . .

". . . Most emphatically he was no Henri Rousseau. He lacked the Douanier's imaginative invention and his uninhibited inspiration. What fascinated sophisticated connoisseurs and influenced purposeful painters in both Rousseau and Utrillo was the genuine innocence of the eye and the simplified pictorial statement felt by both men to be self sufficient. . . ." (Duncan Phillips, Introduction to the catalogue of the Utrillo exhibition, Phillips Gallery, Washington 1953–54).

Collection: Galerie Lepoutre, Paris; Adolphe Basler, Paris; Sam Salz, New York.

Exhibited: Exposition d'Oeuvres de Maurice Utrillo, Galerie Lepoutre, December 5–24, 1919, number 30 as "Village de Sarcelles (S. et O.)"; *Trends in European Painting 1880–1930,* The Century Association, New York, February 2–March 31, 1949, number 14, reproduced in the catalogue; *Works of Art Belonging to Alumnae,* Smith College Museum of Art, Northampton, Massachusetts, May–June 1950, number 80; *The Best Period of Utrillo,* The Phillips Gallery, Washington, December 6, 1953–January 11, 1954, number 2.

References: Maurice Utrillo, by Francis Carco, Paris 1921, reproduced page 21; *Utrillo,* by Adolphe Tabarant, Paris 1926, reproduced page 20; *L'Oeuvre complet de Maurice Utrillo,* by Paul Pétridès, Paris 1959, Volume I, page 263, plate 213.

52

Maurice Utrillo 1883-1955

53 BASILIQUE DE SAINT DENIS

Oil on board, 27 × 17

(1910)

Signed lower right, "Maurice Utrillo V."

This painting bears the influence of Pissarro which Maurice Raynal[1] has noted. "On a hopelessly dirty palette he mixed gum plaster and egg-shells into his whites to obtain tonalities of a wonderful freshness and luminosity. What is the explanation of Utrillo's gift? It seems most mysterious. For in his best works there is evidence of a carefully thought-out design, of a plastic discipline such as the impressionists never knew, although some people claim that he was originally inspired by them. Nor is it correct to present him as a realistic observer of the picturesque side of Montmartre, as an expert on its wicked by-ways and the texture of crumbling walls. None of this was ever in his mind, for originally Utrillo had no clear-cut intentions. He could paint just as well from picture post-card views of cathedrals or villages that he had never seen.

"The most plausible explanation of Utrillo's incredible gift is to be found in a kind of unconscious automatism. If my memory serves me well, Utrillo's movements as he painted were involuntary and never deliberate . . . With Utrillo the act of painting seems to have been as much an automatic action as say with a pianist who improvises while thinking of something else."[2]

[1] Maurice Raynal, "Maurice Utrillo", *History of Modern Painting From Picasso to Surrealism*, Geneva 1950, page 30.
[2] *ibid*, pages 30–31.

Collection: Galerie Lepoutre, Paris; Adolphe Basler, Paris; Alfred Daber, Paris; Sam Salz, New York; Leigh Block, Chicago.

Exhibited: Exposition Maurice Utrillo V. De 1905 à 1925, Galerie H. Fiquet et Cie., Paris, May 1925, number 18, reproduced in the catalogue; *Oeuvres importantes de Maurice Utrillo*, Galerie André Schoeller, Paris, May 24–June 16, 1934, number 8 as "L'Eglise abbatiale de Saint-Denis", reproduced in the catalogue; *The Best Period of Utrillo*, The Phillips Gallery, Washington, December 6, 1953–January 11, 1954, number 5.

References: Maurice Utrillo, by Adolphe Basler, Paris 1929, reproduced on the cover; *Maurice Utrillo V.*, by Adolphe Basler, Paris 1931, reproduced page 2; *L'Oeuvre complet de Maurice Utrillo*, by Paul Pétridès, Paris 1959, Volume I, page 263, plate 211.

Maurice. Utrillo. V.

Jean Metzinger 1883-1956

54 STILL LIFE

Oil on canvas, $32\frac{1}{2}$ × 24

(1914)

Signed lower right, "Metzinger"

"Despite the fact that Gleizes and Metzinger always denied it, there can be no question of the influence of Picasso and Braque on their art, . . . although their solutions of similar problems differed in some respects . . . Most characteristic of their type of Cubism, however, was the retention of the anecdotal theme; to their mind, the predominance of the object over the subject sufficed to ensure the authenticity of the work as a whole . . .

"To sum up: this type of Cubism produces less the impression of a genuinely revolutionary form of expression than one of a call to order or a régime of austerity. It reaffirms the primacy of the painting itself over its anecdotal or emotive content, but without wholly abandoning the spatial and figurative system deriving from the Renaissance." (Guy Habasque, *Cubism*, Geneva 1959, pages 99–100.)

Collection: Mme. Simon Heller, Paris; Sidney Janis Gallery, New York.

Exhibited: Selection of French Art, Sidney Janis Gallery, New York, February 28–April 9, 1955.

Amedeo Modigliani 1884-1920

55 NU AU COLLIER (Nude with Necklace)

Oil on canvas, $36\frac{1}{4} \times 24$

(1917)

Signed at upper right, "Modigliani"

"Modigliani's most ambitious paintings are his nudes – those images of women lying naked, aggressive and pleased, the tension of frank moment in their faces and animal pride. They are in fact the nudest of nudes, the absolute contradiction of Redon's dictum: 'The painter who paints a nude woman, leaving in our mind the idea that she is going to dress herself immediately, is not an intellectual.' One feels that Modigliani's models have flung off their clothes, eager for the artist's admiration and utterly unrestrained. These are (let us be candid) erotic nudes for the most part, though dignified by convictions of style. If we compare them with Manet's *Olympia,* so scandalous in its time, we see that the last vestiges of allegorical disguise have been abandoned; a Bauderlairian atmosphere of sin has been replaced by blunt stress on precisely the physical realities that earlier art had usually moderated or concealed. Modigliani's women are not the grown-up cherubs of which the eighteenth century was fond. They are adult, sinuous, carnal and real, the final stage in the sequence from Giorgione's *Concert Champêtre* to Manet's *Dejeuner sur l'Herbe* and on to Lautrec and his contemporaries. Yet whereas a certain picturesqueness of evil attaches to Lautrec's works, and indeed to those of many modern artists from Rops to Pascin, Modigliani's sensuality is clear and delighted, like that of Ingres but less afraid. His nudes are an emphatic answer to his Futurist countrymen who, infatuated with the machine, considered the subject outworn and urged its suppression for a period of ten years." (James Thrall Soby, introduction to the catalogue of the Modigliani exhibition, The Museum of Modern Art, New York, 1951, pages 13–15.)

Collection: Léopold Zborowski, Paris; Jacques Netter, Paris; Etiénne Bignou, Paris; A. J. McNeill Reid, London; Mrs. S. Kaye, London; Alex Reid & Lefevre, Ltd., London.

Exhibited: Paintings by Modigliani, The Lefevre Galleries, London, March 1929, number 14; *Paintings by Amedeo Modigliani,* De Hauke and Co., New York, October 21–November 9, 1929, number 29 as "Seated Nude", reproduced in the catalogue; *Trente Ans de Peinture Française,* Galerie de Centaure, Brussels, June 1930, number 37, reproduced in the catalogue; *Nineteenth and Twentieth Century French Painting,* Glasgow, October 1930, number 23; *Amedeo Modigliani,* Demotte, Inc., New York, November 1931, number 8; *Masterpieces by 20th Century French Painters, "L'Ecole de Paris",* The Lefevre Galleries, London, January–February 1932, number 21; *Modigliani,* Palais des Beaux-Arts, Brussels, November 1933, number 38; *The Tragic Painters,* The Lefevre Galleries, London, June 1938, number 7; *Summer Loan Show,* Metropolitan Museum of Art, New York, July–August 1950; *New York Private Collections,* The Museum of Modern Art, June 26 – September 12, 1951.

References: Modigliani, Sa Vie et son Oeuvre by André Salmon, Paris 1926, plate 20; *Modigliani,* by Arthur Pfannstiel, Paris 1929, page 41 of the Catalogue Présumé; "Modigliani", by Adolphe Basler, *Kunst und Künstler,* June 1930, reproduced page 356; "Amedeo Modigliani," by F. Neugass, *Deutsche Kunst und Dekoration,* January 1931, reproduced page 239; "Modigliani the Fated", by Maurice Sachs, *Creative Art,* February 1932, reproduced page 98; *Vente de la Collection "L'Art Moderne", Lucerne (Suisse),* Paris, June 20, 1935, number 43, reproduced facing page 19; *Amedeo Modigliani,* by G. Scheiwiller, Milan 1936, plate X; *Time,* August 27, 1951, reproduced page 79 in color; *Modigliani,* by Gotthard Jedlicka, Erlenbach-Munich, 1953, plate 29 facing page 48; *Modigliani et son Oeuvre,* by Arthur Pfannstiel, Paris 1956, catalogued page 139, number 259; *Amedeo Modigliani,* by Ambrogio Ceroni, Milan 1958, page 61, number 121, plate 121.

55

Amedeo Modigliani 1884-1920

56 PORTRAIT OF SOUTINE

Pencil on paper, $13\frac{7}{8} \times 10\frac{1}{8}$

(1917)

Signed lower right, "Modigliani"

There is another pencil drawing of Soutine by Modigliani in the collection of Mr. and Mrs. J. W. Alsdorf of Chicago.

"Chaim Soutine was one of Modigliani's intimate friends during the years 1916–19 during which he lived in Montmartre. Modigliani was one of the first to recognize the extraordinary talent of the younger artist. In 1918, he painted several portraits of Soutine, one in the Chester Dale collection, another in the J. Netter collection, Paris. A third portrait was painted on the door which separated Soutine's atelier from his own at no. 3, rue Joseph-Bara."[1]

". . . Modigliani's passion was for the human face and figure. We know now that he tried his hand once or twice at landscape. His hand alone was in these attempts, and there is no evidence that still life, the preferred theme of the Cubists, ever interested him seriously. He really loved only human subjects; the head, the full figure, nearly always presented singly. . . . In his intensity of individual characterization, Modigliani holds a fairly solitary place in his epoch. One senses in his finest pictures a unique and forceful impact from the sitter, an atmosphere of special circumstance, not to recur. But he was far from being simply a realist. On the contrary, he solved repeatedly one of modern portraiture's most difficult problems: how to express objective truth in terms of the artist's private compulsion. The vigor of his style burns away over-localized fact. Indeed, his figures at times have the fascination of ventriloquists' dummies. They are believeable and wholly in character, yet they would be limp and unimagineable without his guiding animation."[2]

[1] "Drawings by Amedeo Modigliani from the Alsdorf Collection" exhibition, Chicago 1955, number 18.
[2] James Thrall Soby in the introduction to the catalogue of the Modigliani exhibition, The Museum of Modern Art, New York, 1951, page 10.

Collection: Jacob M. Goldschmidlt, Paris; Perls Galleries, New York.

Reference: Catalogue de Tableaux Modernes, Aquarelles, Pastels, Gouaches et Dessins, Paris, February 23, 1949, number 44 bis, as "Portrait de Soutine assis".

Roger de la Fresnaye 1885-1925

57 PAYSAGE DE MEULAN

Oil on canvas, $23\frac{1}{2} \times 28\frac{1}{4}$

(1911–12)

Signed lower right, "R de la Fresnaye"

"Of greater interest [than the Joan of Arc] is the series of landscapes La Fresnaye painted during the winter of 1911–12 at Meulan and La Ferté-sous-Jouarre. In these he employed to good effect the precepts of Cézanne and, though the color orchestration is less rich than the master's, the formal structure is very similar. The composition is built up in successive planes, creating depth, and air circulates freely between them, thanks to variations in the intensity of the light." (Guy Habasque, *Cubism*, Geneva 1959, page 115.)

Collection: John Quinn, New York; Marcel Kapférer, Paris; Carstairs Gallery, New York.

Exhibited: Le Cubisme 1907–1914, Musée National d'Art Moderne, Paris, January 30–April 9, 1953, number 91.

References: John Quinn 1870–1925, Catalogue of Collection of Paintings, Water Colors, Drawings & Sculpture, Huntington, New York 1926, reproduced page 54 as "Landscape with Chimney"; *Cubism,* by Guy Habasque, Geneva 1959, page 115, reproduced in color page 114.

57

Juan Gris 1887-1927

58 VIOLON ET GUITARE

Oil on canvas, 39½ × 25¾

(1913)

Unsigned

"In August, 1913, Gris and his wife joined Picasso at Céret near the Spanish border. They remained until November. This was the first time Gris had left Paris since his arrival in 1906. He was delighted by the change and perhaps also, despite his persistent disclaimers of any interest in his native land, by his proximity to Spain. At any rate, during his month at Céret he worked superbly, producing such works as the *Violin and Guitar*, which he describes in a letter to Kahnweiler as his own favorite up to that point . . .

"Though Gris' contribution to analytical cubism had been his own and admirable, there can be no doubt that he welcomed the technical and stylistic expansion which synthetic cubism allowed him. The *Violin and Guitar* of 1913 is daring in color. But its pyramidal maze of forms based on musical instruments is compelling. Indeed, the taut, elegant and inevitable contours of the violin had more persistent meaning for Gris than for his fellow cubists. (Soby, *Gris*, page 26.)

Collection: Galerie Kahnweiler, Paris; Comte and Comtesse de Chambrun, Paris; Balaÿ et Carré, Paris; Jacques Seligmann & Co., New York.

Exhibited: Exposition Juan Gris, Galerie Simon, Paris, March 20–April 5, 1923, number 4; *Retrospective Loan Exposition Juan Gris*, Jacques Seligmann & Co., Inc., New York, November 21–December 10, 1938, number 12, plate 12; *Juan Gris Retrospective Exhibition*, Arts Club of Chicago, January 3–27, 1939, number 28; *Color and Space in Modern Art since 1900*, Mortimer Brandt Gallery, New York, February 19–March 18, 1944, number 12; *Four Spaniards: Dali, Gris, Miro, Picasso*, The Institute of Contemporary Art, Boston, January 24–March 3, 1946, number 20; *Juan Gris*, Buchholz Gallery, New York, April 1–26, 1947, number 1; *A Retrospective Exhibition of the Works of Juan Gris*, The Cincinnati Modern Art Society, Cincinnati Art Museum, April 30–May 31, 1948, number 9; *Some Paintings from Alumnae Collections*, Smith College Museum of Art, Northampton, Massachusetts, June 1948; *Summer Loan Show*, Metropolitan Museum of Art, New York, July–August 1950; *New York Private Collections*, The Museum of Modern Art, New York, June 26–September 12, 1951; *Juan Gris*, Berner Kunstmuseum, Bern, October 29, 1955–January 2, 1956, number 11; *Juan Gris*, Biennale di Venezia, June 19–October 21, 1956, page 253, number 6; *European Masters of Our Time*, Museum of Fine Arts, Boston, October 10 – November 17, 1957, number 42, reproduced plate 20; *Juan Gris*, The Museum of Modern Art, New York, April 9 – June 1, 1958, reproduced in color page 29.

References: Catalogue des Tableaux, Aquarelles, Gouaches & Dessins . . . Composant la Collection de la Galerie Kahnweiler, Paris, July 4, 1922, number 96; *Juan Gris*, by Daniel-Henry Kahnweiler, Paris 1946, plate IX facing page 48; *Juan Gris, His Life and Work*, by Daniel-Henry Kahnweiler, New York 1947, plate 8; "La Présence de Juan Gris", P. G. Bruguière, *Cahiers d'Art*, volume 26, 1951, reproduced page 117; *Letters of Juan Gris 1913–1927*, Collected by Daniel-Henry Kahnweiler and Translated and Edited by Douglas Cooper, London 1956, page 2, number III, to Daniel-Henry Kahnweiler, dated Céret, September 17, 1913: "This is to tell you also that I am about to send off 5 pictures which I have finished: *The Bullfighter, The Banker. The Guitar* ! ! !, *Landscape* and *Violin and Guitar* ! ! ! ! ! Tell me particularly what you think of the two last: *Violin* and *Landscape*? I have worked especially hard on the latter and cannot really judge it. The *Violin* is the one I like best . . .": page 3, number IV, "Today I am sending you the 5 pictures I mentioned a few days ago."; "Juan Gris en Suisse", by John Richardson, *XXe Siècle*, January 1956, reproduced page 63; *XIX Festival Internazionale di Musica Contemporanea*, Venice, September 11–22, 1956, reproduced in color on the cover of the catalogue; "Juan Gris", by Georg Schmidt, *Das Kunstwerk*, January 1958, reproduced page 7; *Cubism: A History and an Analysis 1907–1914*, by John Golding, New York 1959, page 131, plate 47A; *Cubism*, by Guy Habasque, Geneva 1959, page 69: "While we must admit that some of his 1912 canvases may seem a little dry or theory-ridden, *Three Cards* (Hermann Rupf Collection, Bern) and *Violin and Guitar* (Ralph Colin Collection, New York) unquestionably rank among the major achievements of Cubism."

Juan Gris 1887-1927

59 LIVRE, PIPE ET VERRES (Book, Pipe and Glasses)

Oil on canvas, 28⅞ × 36

1915

Signed on back upper left, "Juan Gris 3-15"

"If Gris' mood was almost relentingly black in 1915, as his letters attest, his paintings through some blissful irony became more opulent than ever before, and the strange words which Bernard Dorival had applied to his art - 'haughty dryness of design, miserly economy of palette' – are singularly inappropriate. Consider for example, the *Book, Pipe and Glasses* and *The Package of Quaker Oats.* Between them they typify the expressive flexibility of Gris' technique at this time. The main surfaces of the former picture have a tortoise-shell evenness and luminosity; the latter is richly encrusted and in some areas so heavily modeled in depth as to approach bas-relief. In color both images are the opposite of 'miserly'; they are, on the contrary, fearless and vivid. Gris was too decisive a personality to have feared vulgarity, and the violet, rose, green and blue passages in *Book, Pipe and Glasses* achieve a memorable cacophony." (Soby, *Gris*, page 40.)

Collection: Leonce Rosenberg, Paris; Dr. G. F. Reber, Lausanne; Paul de Frassari Adamidi-Bey, Geneva; Georges Moos, Geneva.

Exhibited: Juan Gris, Kunsthaus Zürich, April 2–26, 1933, number 51 as "Le Moulin à Café"; *Juan Gris*, Buchholz Gallery, New York, January–February 1950, number 7, reproduced in the catalogue; *Works of Art Belonging to Alumnae*, Smith College Museum of Art, Northampton, Massachusetts, May–June 1950, number 48; *Summer Loan Show*, Metropolitan Museum of Art, New York, July–August 1950; *New York Private Collections*, The Museum of Modern Art, New York, June 26–September 12, 1951; *Inaugural Exhibition*, Fort Worth Art Center, October 8–31, 1954, number 38, reproduced in the catalogue; *Paintings from Private Collections*, The Museum of Modern Art, New York, May 31–September 5, 1955; *Juan Gris*, Berner Kunstmuseum, Bern, October 29, 1955 – January 2, 1956, number 24, reproduced in the catalogue; *Festival of Art* (Benefit Federation of Jewish Philanthropies of New York), Waldorf-Astoria Hotel, New York, October 29–November 1, 1957, number 71; *Juan Gris*, The Museum of Modern Art, New York, April 9–June 1, 1958, page 48; reproduced in color page 49. Also shown at The Minneapolis Institute of Arts, June 24–July 24, 1958 and San Francisco Museum of Arts, August 11–September 14, 1958 and Los Angeles County Museum, September 29–October 26, 1958.

References: Juan Gris ou Le Goût Solennel, by Douglas Cooper, Geneva 1949, plate 7 in color; *Art News*, February 1950, reproduced in color page 19; "Rockefeller, Whitney, Senior, Odets, Colin", by Henry McBride, *Art News*, Summer 1951, page 36; "Juan Gris at Berne", by John Golding, *The Burlington Magazine*, December 1955, page 384; *The New York Times Book Review*, December 2, 1956, reproduced page 3; *Cubism: A History and an Analysis 1907–1914*, by John Golding, New York 1959, page 134, plate 50A.

59

Juan Gris 1887-1927

60 STILL LIFE – TABLE IN A SIDEWALK CAFE

Oil on canvas, $16\frac{1}{4} \times 10\frac{3}{4}$

(1915–16)

Signed lower left, "Juan Gris"

This is one of the few paintings in which Gris combined his favorite subject of still life with the open air.

"At some point during 1915 Gris must have become especially interested in atmospheric effects. The interest is apparent in the magnificent *Still Life before an Open Window: Place Ravignon*" (in the Arensberg Collection now in the Philadelphia Museum of Art) "in which the street scene in the central background is bathed in a blue light. This light filters indoors in arbitrary shafts to deepen and solidify the forms of a complex still life that includes a bottle of Médoc, a fruit bow, a book, a carafe and a copy of *Le Journal* – the newspaper which appears so often in Gris' art." (Compare the present painting.) "The problem of combining an outdoor view with an interior scene has been faced by innumerable artists throughout the centuries . . ." (Soby, *Gris*, page 50.)

Collection: Leonce Rosenberg, Paris; Baron Napoleon Gourgaud, Paris; Galerie Jeanne Bucher, Paris; Valentine Gallery, New York.

Exhibited: Juan Gris, Buchholz Gallery, New York, April 1–26, 1947, number 7; *A Retrospective Exhibition of the Works of Juan Gris*, The Cincinnati Modern Art Society, The Cincinnati Art Museum, April 30–May 31, 1948, number 18; *Picasso, Gris, Miro – The Spanish Masters of Twentieth Century Painting*, San Francisco Museum of Art, September 14–October 17, 1948, and Portland Art Museum, Oregon, October 26–November 28, 1948, number 28; reproduced in the catalogue page 79; *Juan Gris*, Berner Kunstmuseum, Bern, October 29, 1955–January 2, 1956, number 32 as "Verre et Journal".

LE J
NAL

Juan Gris 1887-1927

61 NATURE MORTE

Oil on wood, $29\frac{3}{4} \times 40\frac{1}{2}$

1917

Signed lower right, "Juan Gris 5-17"

This painting in itself is like a small Gris retrospective. The bottle and goblet in the lower left corner are painted in the manner of 1911 (compare the *Still Life* in the Collection of The Museum of Modern Art, New York, reproduced in Soby, *Gris*, page 16). The yellow dotted area in the upper center and the black-and-white element below it are typical of 1915–16 (compare paintings reproduced in Soby, *Gris*, pages 54, 55, 56 and 66). The checker board and the blue grill work in the upper right and the long triangular shadows in the center are all elements which appear in the well-known *Still Life before an Open Window: Place Ravignan*, 1915 (Arensberg Collection, Philadelphia Museum of Art, reproduced in Soby, *Gris*, page 53). The painting itself is dated May 1917. The presence in one painting of these various elements has caused a critic to question its "logic". Other critics have found it "handsome", "rich in color" and notable for its "purity".

One can only speculate on what was in Gris' mind when he produced this work. He may well have been consciously reviewing his "artist's life" in an autobiographical mood very much in the manner of Richard Strauss in *Ein Heldenleben* in which he quotes musically numerous passages from his own earlier works including *Till Eulenspiegel*, *Don Juan*, *Don Quixote* and others. This suggestion is borne out to some extent by Soby's comments. "Oddly enough, the change toward complication in Gris' paintings of 1917 took place at a moment when the artist looked backward to re-examine his early work as a cubist. The inexplicable objects at the left of *The Chessboard* [Collection of The Museum of Modern Art, New York] though new in inventiveness of iconographical identity, are somewhat comparable to the windswept forms that had been Gris' personal contribution to cubism in his paintings of 1911 and 1912. One therefore assumes that the painter was unusually introspective during the early months of 1917 and that he may have wished both to review the beginnings of his mature art and to extend his still-life vocabulary through the inclusion of enigma and paradox." (Soby, *Gris*, page 78.)

Collection: Leonce Rosenberg, Paris; Galerie de L'Effort Moderne, Paris; Léon Kochnitsky, Paris; Galerie de Beaune, Paris; Walter P. Chrysler, Jr., New York; Valentine Gallery, New York; The Museum of Modern Art, New York, Gift of Mr. and Mrs. Ralph F. Colin.

Exhibited: Gris Retrospective Exhibition, The Arts Club of Chicago, January 3–27, 1939, number 7; *Classic and Romantic Traditions in Abstract Painting*, Circulating Exhibition of The Museum of Modern Art, New York, 1939–40; *Collection of Walter P. Chrysler, Jr.*, The Virginia Museum of Fine Arts, Richmond, January 16–March 4, 1941, and The Philadelphia Museum of Art, March 29–May 11, 1941, number 58, reproduced in the catalogue; *School of Paris*, Valentine Gallery, New York, March 25–April 13, 1946, number 10; *Juan Gris*, Buchholz Gallery, New York, April 1–26, 1947, number 9, reproduced in the catalogue; *A Retrospective Exhibition of the Works of Juan Gris*, The Cincinnati Modern Art Society, Cincinnati Art Museum, April 30–May 31, 1948, number 22; *Some Paintings from Alumnae Collections*, Smith College Museum of Art, Northampton, Massachusetts, June 1948, reproduced in *Smith Alumnae Quarterly*, August 1948, page 192.

References: Tableaux Modernes, Hotel Drouôt, Paris, May 6, 1932, number 87; reproduced in the catalogue; "341 Documents of Modern Art: The Chrysler Collection", by Alfred M. Frankfurter, *Art News*, January 18, 1941, reproduced page 9; "Eine Lanze für Juan Gris", by Werner Haftmann, *Die Zeit* (Hamburg), June 3, 1948, reproduced page 5; *Malerei im 20. Jahrhundert*, by Werner Haftmann, Munich 1955, reproduced page 129 in the volume of plates.

61

Juan Gris 1887-1927

62 VIOLON ET CLARINETTE

Oil on canvas, 15 × 24

1921

Signed lower right, "Juan Gris 9-21" *and inscribed lower left,* "Violon et Clarinette"

"There has been a considerable amount of theorizing as to why musical instruments meant so much to the cubists in general, and the musical inclinations of Picasso, Braque, Gris and the others have perhaps been over-stressed. It seems to the writer more plausible to assume that the cubists, in their arduous task of reappraising everyday appearances through a new and revolutionary plastic system, liked the violin, the guitar and the mandolin because the basic design of these instruments had undergone very little change for several centuries. Their challenge to the cubists was therefore all the more explicit. At any rate, the violin's complexity of design appears in a sense to symbolize the conscientious intellectuality which Gris brought to cubist research. This is not to say, of course, that he was more intellectual than his two great colleagues. But he was, one assumes, more metaphysical in his conception of how the common-place and the traditional could become the point of departure for a new order in painting." (Soby, *Gris,* pages 26 and 27.)

Collection: Galerie Simon, Paris; Alfred Flechtheim, Berlin; The Mayor Gallery, London; Curt Valentin Gallery, New York.

Exhibited: Juan Gris, The Mayor Gallery, London, November 1936, number 16; *Juan Gris,* Buchholz Gallery, New York, April 1–26, 1947, number 14, reproduced in the catalogue; *A Retrospective Exhibition of the Works of Juan Gris,* The Cincinnati Modern Art Society, Cincinnati Art Museum, April 30–May 31, 1948, number 43; *Cubism,* Buchholz Gallery, New York, April 5–30, 1949, number 14; *Juan Gris,* Buchholz Gallery, New York, January 16–February 11, 1950, number 23; *Closing Exhibition,* Curt Valentin Gallery, New York, June 1955, number 42; *Juan Gris,* Berner Kunstmuseum, Bern, October 29, 1955–January 2, 1956, number 92.

62

Juan Gris 1887-1927

63 COMPOTIER ET GUITARE (Fruit-dish and Guitar)

Oil on canvas, $19\frac{3}{4} \times 28\frac{3}{4}$

1923

Signed lower left, "Juan Gris 1923"

"It is unquestionably true that Gris completed some excellent works during the final seven years of his life . . . Nevertheless, one questions whether Gris was ever again after 1920 as consistently inspired an artist as he had been before, perhaps due in part to chronic illness, in part to his absorbtion for a time in stage design . . . In Kahnweiler's opinion the reservations many of us feel about some of Gris' late work can be ascribed to 'an old misunderstanding of cubism.' The theory is rather hard to credit in that many of Gris' most fervent admirers have been devoted to the cubist movement and a few of them have made it the subject of prolonged research." (Soby, *Gris,* page 96.)

Collection: Galerie Simon, Paris; Samuel Lewis, New York; Sally Lewis, Portland, Maine; Douglas Cooper, London; Walter P. Chrysler, Jr., New York.

Exhibited: Juan Gris, Galerie Simon, Paris, March 20–April 5, 1923, number 52; *Spanish Art,* L'Art Contemporain, Antwerp, April 1923; *Juan Gris,* Marie Harriman Gallery, New York, February 1932, number 16; *Collection of Walter P. Chrysler, Jr.,* The Virginia Museum of Fine Arts, Richmond, January 16–March 4, 1941, and The Philadelphia Museum of Art, March 29–May 11, 1941, number 60; *A Retrospective Exhibition of the Works of Juan Gris,* The Cincinnati Modern Art Society, Cincinnati Art Museum, April 30–May 31, 1948, number 51; *Picasso, Gris, Miro – The Spanish Masters of Twentieth Century Painting,* San Francisco Museum of Art, September 14–October 17, 1948, and Portland Art Museum, Oregon, October 26–November 28, 1948, number 39, reproduced in the catalogue page 85; *Juan Gris,* Berner Kunstmuseum, Bern, October 29, 1955–January 2, 1956, number 98, reproduced in the catalogue; *Cubism in Retrospect 1911–1929,* Denver Art Museum, January 22–February 22, 1959, number 31, reproduced in the catalogue.

References: "Der gegenwärtige Stand der Malerei in Frankreich", by Adolphe Basler, *Jahrbuch der jungen Kunst,* 1923, reproduced page 332; *Juan Gris,* by Daniel Henry (pseud. of Daniel-Henry Kahnweiler), Leipzig and Berlin 1929, plate 18; *French and other Modern Paintings . . . From the Collection of Walter P. Chrysler, Jr.,* New York, April 11, 1946, number 28, reproduced in the catalogue page 16; *Juan Gris,* by Daniel-Henry Kahnweiler, New York 1947, plate 81 as "Fruit-dish and Guitar"; *Letters of Juan Gris 1913–1927,* Collected by Daniel-Henry Kahnweiler and Translated and Edited by Douglas Cooper, London 1956, page 150, number CLXXII, to Gertrude Stein and dated, Boulogne s/Seine, December 27, 1922: "I'm rather satisfied with my latest pictures": and again, page 152, number CLXXVI, to Gertrude Stein, dated February 27, 1923: "I am working hard to finish some pictures I have begun. As I have about ten here, I would like to show them to you before they are exhibited."

63

Kurt Schwitters 1887–1948

64 EERS

Paper collage, $6\frac{3}{4} \times 5\frac{1}{2}$

1947

Signed lower left, "Kurt Schwitters 1947" *and inscribed lower right*, "EERS"

"Of those artists to use *Collage* as a medium in XXth Century Art, Kurt Schwitters has been the most persistent. In his earliest works of the Dada period (1919–1923) *Collage* was mainly his technique, and continued to be until his death in England in 1948.

"Whether we attribute the use of *Collage* in his work to psychological or sociological factors, or characterize his technique as cubist, dada or abstract, the result was always of highest esthetic merit. Scraps of paper which he used were selected from the world of waste, retrieved and given an artistic life of their own. Despite the usual small format of the pictures – sometimes only a few centimeters – they are monumental.

"In his lifetime Schwitters was recognized only by a small coterie. Today he is a great inspiration to younger artists who are finding *Collage* more and more an authentic medium of XXth Century artistic expression." (Introduction to the catalogue of the Schwitters exhibition, Sidney Janis Gallery, New York, 1959.)

Collection: Curt Valentin Gallery, New York; Sidney Janis Gallery, New York.

TO
L.M
9
2/-
THOMAS

Josef Albers 1888-

65 HOMAGE TO THE SQUARE – RESTRAINED GLOW

Oil on board, 24 × 24

(1951)

Unsigned

"The square has then existed for some time as a basic problem in modern painting, but Albers has now endowed it with a new character. In its earlier appearances it had been treated as a fundamental, absolute principle of design, almost in a Platonic sense. For Mondrian it was one of the primary forms with which he hoped to communicate his experience of ultimate reality. For Albers, on the other hand, whose search for new combinations of color never ceases in contrast to Modrian's satisfaction with three, the colored square is not a static end in itself but an active tool in his search for a reality which is constantly changing. Albers's *Squares* are never at rest, they are never flat, they are always undergoing ceaseless transformation of size and shape and distance as the properties of colors in combination endlessly create different optical experiences. A new and unexpected dimension is given to many of the *Squares* by changes in the character and kind of light in which they are seen. They are different in daylight from what they are at night, and those who have had the privilege of living with them know that they are not the same at twilight or at dusk. The witty, delicate, even on occasion poignant subtitles which Albers gives to the *Homages* relate them in an immediate and often unexpected way to our own lives. We may discover that some sources of memory or expectation have been suddenly touched by the serene and sympathetic artistry of these studies in 'relatedness'. Finally, these multiple appearances of temporal change developed upon a constant spacial theme suggest that the philosophical analogy may still hold. The Platonic absolute cherished by the earlier constructive artists has become in Albers's hands an instrument for interpreting with an almost Aristotelian feeling for the organic principles of form the artist's consuming interest in the unending varieties of color instrumentation." (George Heard Hamilton, *Josef Albers, Paintings, Prints, Projects*, Catalogue of an exhibition at Yale University Art Gallery, April 25–June 18, 1956, pages 41–42.)

Collection: Sidney Janis Gallery, New York.

Exhibited: Albers Exhibition, Sidney Janis Gallery, New York, January 1952; *Art Our Children Live With*, The Downtown Gallery, New York, December 9–21, 1957, number 1.

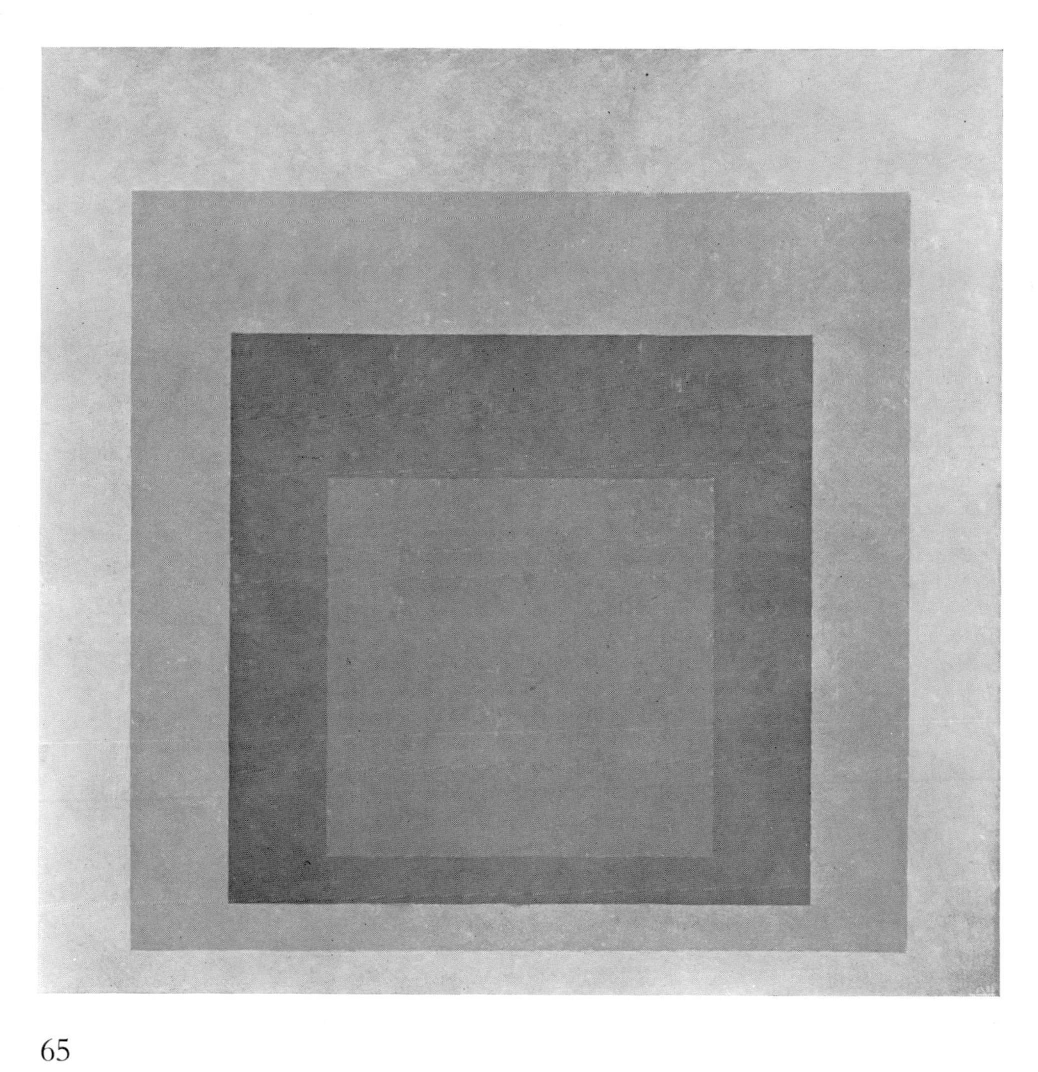

65

Georgio Morandi 1890-

66 STILL LIFE

Oil on canvas, $11\frac{3}{4} \times 15\frac{1}{2}$

(1931)

Signed lower right, "Morandi"

"The artist who profited most by his venture into Metaphysical Painting was the last-comer of the group, Giorgio Morandi, who joined them in 1918. He had never been to Paris, but, gifted with a rare sensitivity, he had sensed intuitively as it were the ideas behind Cubism and Futurism. What he brought to Metaphysical Painting was a wholly personal delicacy of color and a unique purity of form. In Morandi's art the 'revelation of the unknowable', if limited in scope, is inherent in the forms themselves; whereas Carrà and de Chirico hinted at the mystery behind reality by startling combinations of incongruous objects, Morandi finds it in the objects themselves, because of his love for all existing things, even the simplest, such as bottles set in rows and household utensils. And such is his natural modesty and unassertiveness that he makes arrangements of these his leading themes. But the bottles and other objects are transmuted into symphonies of exquisite color, bathed in a light so tenuous that it seems to glance over rather than strike their surfaces, and vibrant with that subtle rhythm which gives Morandi's art its amazing power of suggestion. The contour-lines – that is to say the form – the color and the composition have that supreme *rightness*, inevitability, to which Morandi owes his secure, if hardly won, place in the forefront of Italian art. His renown is world-wide, yet the strange thing is that in private life he is the most provincial of Italian artists; nothing induces him to quit his native city, Bologna." (Lionello Venturi, *Italian Painting from Caravaggio to Modigliani*, Geneva 1951, page 103.)

Collection: Galleria d'Arte del Naviglio, Milan; Curt Valentin Gallery, New York.

67 STILL LIFE

Oil on canvas, 14×16

(1953)

Signed lower left, "Morandi"

Collection: Curt Valentin Gallery, New York.

68 STILL LIFE

Oil on canvas, $11\frac{3}{4} \times 17\frac{3}{4}$

(1953)

Signed lower left, "Morandi"

Collection: Curt Valentin Gallery, New York.

66

67

68

Karl Knaths 1891-

69 COPPER KETTLE

Oil on canvas, 30 × 40

(1950)

Signed lower right, "Karl Knaths"

"In Knaths the lyrical and the logical are indivisible as in Braque. Like Braque he combines sensitiveness and strength. However, the pure aesthetic elegance and classic philosophy of Braque are not in Knaths. Karl's art is like himself, close to nature and the elements. Knaths is a lyrical but never a dramatic Expressionist. His semi-abstract idiom is spontaneous and at times even impetuous and yet never subconscious, never automatism. The artist's hand moves with his mind over the deeply respected picture plane in a freedom acquired through study and discipline. He carries on the tradition of Cézanne but adds to it his personal innovations of line, sensibility and humor. Knaths is a simple man, a man of profound goodness and integrity who reacts to thrills of artistic discovery whether visual or technical with the same zest for nature in its more untamed elements which attracts him to American folk lore. He is dedicated to a life for which he was born with a great purpose – to paint each canvas better and ever better until whatever it was that thrilled his inner eye transcends the colors he knows so well how to mix and manage. There is philosophy and nobility in the artist as in the man." (Paul Mocsanyi, *Karl Knaths*, Washington 1957, page 8.)

Collection: Paul Rosenberg Galleries, New York.

Exhibited: Recent Paintings by Karl Knaths, Paul Rosenberg Galleries, New York, November 5–24, 1951, number 1; *Karl Knaths*, de Cordova and Dana Museum and Park, Lincoln, Massachusetts, November 23, 1952–January 4, 1953, number 11; *Paintings by Karl Knaths from 1946–1953*, Paul Rosenberg Galleries, January 11–30, 1954, number 8; *Art Our Children Live With*, The Downtown Gallery, December 9–21, 1957, number 22; *The Museum and Its Friends*, Whitney Museum of American Art, New York, April 30–June 15, 1958, number 84.

69

Joan Miró 1893-

70 AU CIRQUE

Tempera and oil on canvas, 45 × 34½

1925

Signed lower right, "Miro 1925"

"But fantasy and subjective description were not enough for Miró. He was ever more eager to exceed the limitation of his art. Surrealism pointed the way. For through surrealism's approach he saw the way to break his link with both subjective and objective description, confident that his sound technical training and essential loyalty to painting would protect him against losing sight of the fundamentally pictorial nature of his work.

"The year 1925 saw Miró wipe his canvases practically clean in order to give a final blow to any surviving fetter of reasoned form. He felt the most drastic step possible was the only practical one toward the compassing of the surrealist ideal – the expression of 'the real process of thought . . . thought's dictation, all exercise of thought's reason and every esthetic or moral preoccupation being absent.' *Composition* and *Glove with Face* are two of the early steps toward a new idiom, the direction in which Miró has continued down to the present day. Descriptive forms and the fantastic distortions of them have now disappeared completely. In their place we find masses of color embodying the simplest compositional schemes, symbolic extracts of forms, a complete ideography made credible only through the artist's powerful gift of poetic suggestion." (James Johnson Sweeney, *Joan Miró,* New York 1941, pages 35–36.)

Collection: Valentine Gallery, New York.

Exhibited: Joan Miró, The Museum of Modern Art, New York, November 18, 1941–January 11, 1942, page 35 as "Glove with face", catalogued page 80 and reproduced in the catalogue page 36; *Four Spaniards: Dali, Gris, Miró, Picasso,* The Institute of Contemporary Art, Boston, January 24–March 3, 1946, number 37; *Some Paintings from Alumnae Collections,* Smith College Museum of Art, Northampton, Massachusetts, June 1948; *Picasso, Gris, Miró – The Spanish Masters of Twentieth Century Painting,* San Francisco Museum of Art, September 14–October 17, 1948, and Portland Art Museum, Portland, Oregon, October 26–November 28, 1948, number 47 and reproduced page 99; *Summer Loan Show,* Metropolitan Museum of Art, New York, July–August 1950; *Artists of the Graduate Center,* Busch-Reisinger Museum, Harvard University, January 22–March 4, 1951; *New York Private Collections,* The Museum of Modern Art, New York, June 26–September 12, 1951; *The Struggle for New Form,* World House Galleries, New York (Opening Exhibition) January 22–February 23, 1957, number 54.

Reference: "Rockefeller, Whitney, Senior, Odets, Colin" by Henry McBride, *Art News,* Summer 1951, page 60.

70

Joan Miró 1893-

71 LA POÉTESSE

Gouache on paper, 15 × 18

1940

Signed lower left, "Miro" *and inscribed on the back* "Joan Miró – La Poétesse – Palma de Majorque 31/XII/1940"

On the fall of France, Miró went to Palma, Mallorca, now his permanent home. At the time the war broke out, he "felt a deep desire to escape" and, as he later reported to James Johnson Sweeney in an interview, "I closed myself within myself purposely. The night, music, and the stars began to play a major role in suggesting my paintings."

"The result of this intense withdrawal into himself was a breathtaking series of twenty-three small gouaches, begun at Varangeville and completed at Palma, where he remained until 1942.

"Of these gouaches one was given by the artist to his wife; the remaining twenty-two were shown after the war at the Pierre Matisse Gallery, New York, where they had an immense and well-deserved success. The pictures in the series seem so spontaneous that it comes as a surprise to learn from Miró himself that they were 'exacting both technically and physically', and that each took at least a month to produce. The artist adds that he was most of all intent on compositional balance. 'I would set out with no preconceived idea. A few forms suggested here would call for other forms elsewhere to balance them. These in turn demanded others . . . I would take it (each gouache) up day after day to paint in other tiny spots, stars, washes, infinitesimal dots of color in order to achieve a full and complex equilibrium.'

"It must be admitted that seldom in his career has Miró achieved a more intricate compositional balance than in the 'constellations', of which three of the finest are *The Poetess, Awakening at Dawn*" [see number 72 of this catalogue] "and *Beautiful Bird Revealing the Unknown to a Pair of Lovers.* The series as a whole is extraordinary in quality, and nearly all its pictures have the signature of total conviction. These paintings also have impressive carrying power for works executed on so small a scale; the tiny forms interlock and unravel with a delicious inevitability. . . ." (James Thrall Soby, *Joan Miró,* New York 1959, pages 100 and 106.)

Collection: Pierre Matisse Gallery, New York, from the artist.

Exhibited: Joan Miró, Ceramics 1944, Tempera Paintings 1940–1941, Lithographs 1944, Pierre Matisse Gallery, New York, January 9–February 3, 1945, number 13; *Four Spaniards: Dali, Gris, Miró, Picasso,* The Institute of Contemporary Art, Boston, January 24 – March 3, 1946, number 41; *Works of Art Belonging to Alumnae,* Smith College Museum of Art, Northampton, Massachusetts, May–June 1950, number 61; *New York Private Collections,* The Museum of Modern Art, New York, June 26–September 12, 1951; *Calder-Miró Exhibition,* Contemporary Arts Association of Houston, October 14–November 4, 1951, Miró number 14; *Joan Miró,* XXVII Biennale di Venezia, June 19–October 17, 1954, page 200, number 16 as "Risveglio all'alba"; *Joan Miró Constellations,* Berggruen & Cie, Paris, January–February 1959, a fragment reproduced in color in the catalogue; *Joan Miró,* The Museum of Modern Art, New York, March 18–May 10, 1959, number 76, and the Los Angeles County Museum, June 10–July 26, 1959, number 78.

References: "Miró's Modern Magic" by James Johnson Sweeney, *Town & Country,* April 1945, reproduced in color page 93; *Joan Miró,* by Clement Greenberg, New York 1948, reproduced in color page 81; *Mizue,* Revue Mensuelle des Arts, (Tokyo), February 1953, reproduced in color page 47 as "Poète"; "Form, Function, and Fantasy", *Young Americans,* October 1958 reproduced page 28; "Constellations de Joan Miró", by André Breton, *L'Oeil,* December 1958, reproduced page 55; *Constellations by Joan Miró,* introduction and twenty-two Proses Paralleles by André Breton, New York 1959, plate 13 in color; *Joan Miró* by James Thrall Soby, New York 1959, page 106, reproduced in color page 107; "Miró" by Pierre Schneider, *Horizon,* March 1959 reproduced in color page 77; "Month in Review" by Hilton Kramer, *Arts,* May 1959, reproduced page 48.

71

Joan Miró 1893-

72 LE REVEIL AU PETIT JOUR (Awakening at Dawn)

Gouache on paper, 18 × 15

1941

Signed lower left, "Miro" *and inscribed on the back* "Joan Miró – Le réveil au petit jour – Palma de Marjorque 27/1/1941"

Collection: Pierre Matisse Gallery, New York, from the artist.

Exhibited: Joan Miró, Ceramics 1944, Tempera Paintings 1940–1941, Lithographs 1944, Pierre Matisse Gallery, New York, January 9–February 3, 1945, number 14; *Four Spaniards: Dali, Gris, Miró, Picasso,* The Institute of Contemporary Art, Boston, January 24 – March 3, 1946, number 42; *Some Paintings from Alumnae Collections,* Smith College Museum of Art, Northampton, Massachusetts, June 1948; *Artists of the Graduate Center,* Busch-Reisinger Museum, Harvard University, January 22–March 4, 1951; *Constellations by Joan Miró,* Berggruen & Cie, Paris, January–February 1959; *Joan Miró,* The Museum of Modern Art, New York, March 18 – May 10, 1959, number 79, and Los Angeles County Museum, June 10–July 26, 1959, number 79.

References: "Los ultimos Cuadros de Miró", *Revista Belga* (New York) January 1945, reproduced page 64; *Joan Miró,* by Clement Greenberg, New York 1948, plate LXV, page 104; *Joan Miró,* by Jacques Prévert and G. Ribemont-Dessaignes, Paris 1956, reproduced page 150 as "L'Eveil à l'aube"; *Constellations by Joan Miró,* introduction and twenty-two Proses Paralleles by André Breton, New York 1959, plate 14 in color; *Joan Miró,* by James Thrall Soby, New York 1959, page 106 and reproduced page 104.

72

Joan Miró 1893-

73 PERSONAGES AND STAR

Oil on canvas, $25\frac{1}{2} \times 20$

(1949)

Signed on back, "Miro"

"For all art is essentially play – as all full living is a game that is enjoyed. This is probably the basic explanation of those frail or arid reaches which occasionally appear in the history of art; the failure of art in those times to express and to refresh itself in play. When a culture begins to regard play as something not quite respectable that culture is already facing sterility. To keep an art or culture fertile it must be 'played'.

"Spontaneity and freshness of expression are the objectives of the play-approach in art. These are the characteristics we at once associate with Miró's painting . . .

"In the ease, the vitality and richness of imagination and his sensibility in the exploitation of his medium, we see the product of thirty years severe self-discipline. A freedom won by the imposition of limitations. By play within rules. The play-factor constantly refreshing and rejuvenating the rules of the game, constantly maturing the expression, and by their limitations condensing and enriching it." (James Johnson Sweeney in Introduction to catalogue of the Miró Exhibition at Pierre Matisse Gallery, New York, 1953.)

Collection: Pierre Matisse Gallery, from the artist.

Exhibited: Joan Miró, Pierre Matisse Gallery, New York, March 6–31, 1951, number 7, and reproduced in the catalogue. A letter from Pierre Matisse dated April 5, 1951 to Ralph F. Colin states, "It was the unanimous opinion that your painting by Miró was the best of the whole exhibition"; *Joan Miró*, XXVII Biennale di Venezia, June 19–October 17, 1954, number 23, catalogued page 200 as "Figure".

Reference: Mizue, Revue Mensuelle des Arts (Tokyo), February 1953, reproduced page 17 as "Personnage et l'étoile".

73

Chaim Soutine 1894-1943

74 STILL LIFE WITH SOUP TUREEN

Oil on canvas, 24 × 29

(1916)

Signed lower right, "C. Soutine"

Soutine first came to Paris in 1913. From 1916 to 1919 he lived at *La Ruche*, the "beehive" in Montmartre where his friends included Pascin, Chagall, Lipchitz, Kisling, Zadkine and Modigliani, who was the first to appreciate his remarkable temperament.

"In the earliest work of Soutine which has been preserved, he showed neither a marked academic facility nor any decisive revolutionary purpose. His development was more a matter of intuitive gestation than of deliberate innovation or experiment. As a matter of course, in the art school at Vilna, and at the Beaux-Arts under Cormon, he was taught a kind of nineteenth-century realism, dark and painstaking. There is something of this to be seen in the *Still Life with Tureen*, a rather awkwardly formal arrangement enhanced by luminous whites and warm shadows. . . . In all these *La Ruche* works one perceives only the commencement of the emotional intensity which was soon to follow." (Wheeler, *Soutine*, page 46.)

Collection: Valentine Gallery, New York.

Exhibited: 23 Paintings by Soutine, Valentine Gallery, New York, March 20–April 8, 1939, number 9; *Soutine*, The Museum of Modern Art, New York, November 1, 1950–January 7, 1951, and The Cleveland Museum of Art, January 31–March 18, 1951, catalogued page 112 and reproduced page 36; *Soutine*, Circulating Exhibition of The Museum of Modern Art, New York, 1951–52; *Chaim Soutine*, XXVI Biennale di Venezia, June 14–October 19, 1952, page 181, number 1 as "Natura Morta".

References: Soutine by Monroe Wheeler, New York 1950, page 46, reproduced page 36; "The Cataclysmic World of Chaim Soutine", by Margaret Bruening, *The Art Digest*, November 15, 1950, page 11; *Modigliani, Chagall, Soutine, Pascin: Aspects of Expressionism*, by Paolo d'Ancona, Milan 1952, page 59, reproduced in color page 51; *Soutine*, by Jacques Lassaigne, Paris 1954, reproduced in color plate 2 where it is erroneously placed in another collection; *Soutine et son Temps*, by Emile Szittya, Paris 1955, listed in "Tableau Chronologique" page 114 as "Nature morte à la soupière".

74

Chaim Soutine 1894-1943

75 STILL LIFE WITH CABBAGE

Oil on board, 21 × 17½

(1919)

Signed lower right, "Soutine"

Soutine rarely dated his pictures, indeed, rarely signed them. Many of his "signatures" were added later by friends, dealers and others. His true signature is his work. The dates are fixed only by reference to other established work of the period.

"Soutine, Pascin, Utrillo and Modigliani – they have been grouped together as though violence of temper and proneness to trouble constituted a school of art. In France they are called *les peintres maudits* – painters under a curse. The lives of some post-Impressionists, notably Gauguin and van Gogh, have put in the general mind and in the repertory of journalism about art a concept of melodramatic greatness. Here was another such generation . . .

"Soutine was the least calamitous and least dissipated of the four, but perhaps the saddest. For as his art developed, it offered no distraction from his anxieties, animosities and self-reproach – no escape. Not that he intended any effect of autobiography by means of his art. But from an early age he used his hardship, pessimism and truculence to set a tragic tone for his painting, irrespective of its subject matter. Limiting the themes of his work to conventional categories – still life, landscape, portraiture and picturesque figure-painting – he would always charge his pictures with extreme implications of what he had in mind: violence of nature, universality of hunger, and a peculiar mingling of enthusiasms and antipathies." (Wheeler, *Soutine*, page 31.)

Collection: Max Moos, Geneva, from the artist.

75

Chaim Soutine 1894–1943

76 PEASANT BOY

Oil on canvas, $24\frac{1}{2} \times 21$

(1920–22)

Unsigned

" . . . What we may call the Cagnes style is as effective in the portraits as in the scenes of tree-tops and hill towns. . . .

"These are speaking likenesses of more or less humble persons whom he invested with the poise of royalty, or of those who think themselves royal. Who can tell what Soutine thought of them? Surely he was enthralled by their idiosyncrasy. He caricatured them, but not to amuse himself or to punish them. In the over-powering prostitutes and judges of Rouault, as in the small foxy figures of Daumier, there is satiric purpose, indignation and castigation. But there is nothing of the sort in Soutine. He has no special grievance against anyone; this is pure portraiture. He selects the salient features of these persons, their intensive gaze, outstanding ears, huge interworking hands, and renders them to excess with only summary indication of the body which he then cloaks in the magnificences of the palette. They are unforgettable." (Wheeler, *Soutine*, pages 61 and 65.)

Collection: Léopold Zborowski, Paris; Bignou Gallery, New York.

Exhibited: Soutine, Bignou Gallery, New York, March 22–April 16, 1943, number 10; *Exhibition of Modern Paintings*, Bignou Gallery, New York, January 1945, number 16; *Group Show*, Boston Museum of Fine Arts – Museum School, Boston, March 6–20, 1950; *Summer Loan Show*, Metropolitan Museum of Art, New York, July–August 1950; *Impressionism and Expressionism*, Busch-Reisinger Museum, Harvard University, February 12–March 20, 1954, number 44; *Expressionism 1900–1955*, Walker Art Center, Minneapolis, January 22–March 11, 1956, reproduced in the catalogue: then at The Institute of Contemporary Art, Boston, April 11–May 20: San Francisco Museum of Art, June 6–July 22: Cincinnati Art Museum and Contemporary Arts Center, August 28–September 23: Baltimore Museum of Art, October 9–November 4: Albright Art Gallery, Buffalo, November 16–December 30.

76

Chaim Soutine 1894-1943

77 LANDSCAPE AT CERET

Oil on canvas, $21\frac{1}{4} \times 36\frac{1}{4}$

(1920)

Signed lower right, "Soutine"

"The three years from 1919 to 1922, spent for the most part at Céret, were the most prolific of his life; during this time he painted over two hundred canvases. His accelerated production has been attributed to his alarm at the death of his friend Modigliani, who died in 1920 at the height of his career, ruined by dissipation and distress. . . . The calamitous extinguishment of this artist of great facility and more fortunate background must have caused all of his friends to doubt the feasibility of their wild, artistic way of life, and it is possible that the emotions precipitated by this event expressed themselves in certain tumultous and obscure canvases which Soutine did at the time. . . .

"Of all the phases of Soutine's painting, this is the least legible, the hardest to understand, and the most rapid in experimental transitions. The sombre, interspersed colors of the Céret pictures, the upheavals of ambiguous and repetitious form, constituted a tremendous experiment, a determined research, canvas after canvas." (Wheeler, *Soutine*, pages 50 and 51.)

Collection: Max Moos, Geneva; The Fogg Art Museum, Harvard University, gift of Mr. and Mrs. Ralph F. Colin.

Exhibited: French and American Moderns, Feigl Gallery, New York, December 1950, number 2 as "House by the Hill (Céret)"; *New York Private Collections*, The Museum of Modern Art, New York, June 26–September 12, 1951.

This painting is included in the exhibition at the Knoedler Gallery by permission of The Fogg Art Museum, Harvard University.

77

Chaim Soutine 1894-1943

78 GNARLED TREES

Oil on canvas, 38 × 25

(1921)

Signed lower left, "Soutine"

"Certainly one of the finest of the Céret group is the large upright *Gnarled Trees* with its magical fusing of autumnal reds, greens and yellows. In it there is only one of the sloping architectural patterns; the rest is hillside, bark, twig and bough, all leading upward under the houses with a wavering-like flame."[1]

"One of the earliest descriptive references to Soutine's way of painting also came from Modigliani's lips. By that time the latter was gravely addicted to drugs, as well as alcohol, and as he was commencing a bout of intoxication he remarked, 'Everything dances around me as in a landscape by Soutine'."[2]

[1] Wheeler, *Soutine*, page 56. [2] *ibid*, pages 41 and 42.

Collection: Léopold Zborowski, Paris.

Exhibited: Soutine, The Museum of Modern Art, New York, November 1, 1951–January 7, 1951, and The Cleveland Museum of Art, January 31–March 18, 1951, page 56, catalogued page 112 and reproduced page 49; *Soutine*, A Circulating Exhibition of The Museum of Modern Art, New York, 1951–52; *States of Mind*, Circulating Exhibition of The Museum of Modern Art, New York, 1953, 1954, 1955, 1956.

Reference: Notable Modern French and Other Paintings. Property of J. J. Puritz . . . and Other Owners, New York January 17–18, 1945, number 146 as "Gnarled Tree".

Chaim Soutine 1894-1943

79 GLADIOLAS

Oil on canvas, $32\frac{1}{2} \times 23\frac{3}{4}$

(1919 or 1921–23)

Signed upper right, "Soutine"

"Another subject which occupied him for a while at *La Ruche* was gladioli. He painted several canvases of more or less the same vaseful, and the point of his fascination and research in them all seems to have been the play of thick but sinuous stems and flaring red blossoms. It may not have been so much the true forms of the leaves and petals which appealed to him as the blood-redness, fire-redness, which he rendered like little licking flames."[1]

"In 1928, Waldemar George pointed out that the shock of Soutine's way of painting was not so much a matter of form, deformation and malformation, as a certain wildness of rhythm loosed on the canvas, twisting in every lineament of nature and human nature; 'It bends and shakes his figures as though they had St. Vitus' dance. Harmonious still lifes, flowers and fruits, it reduces to rags and tatters. Houses oscillate on their foundations and move ardently hither and thither in the landscape, turning it topsy-turvy as in a series of seismic shocks'."[2]

[1] Wheeler, *Soutine,* page 46. [2] *ibid,* page 48.

Collection: Valentine Gallery, New York.

Exhibited: Soutine, Circulating Exhibition of The Museum of Modern Art, New York, 1951–52; *Still Life and the School of Paris,* Pierre Matisse Gallery, New York, December 1952, number 19 and reproduced in the catalogue; *Soutine,* Perls Galleries, New York, November 2–December 5, 1953, number 2; *Magic of Flowers in Painting,* Wildenstein Gallery, New York, April 13–May 15, 1954, number 75; *Flowers in Art,* Leonid Kipnis Gallery, Westport, Connecticut, April 15–29, 1955.

Reference: "Flowers and Realism", by Jack Tworkow, *Art News,* May 1954, reproduced page 23.

79

Chaim Soutine 1894-1943

80 THE APPRENTICE

Oil on canvas, 39 × 27

(1922)

Signed lower right, "Soutine"

"For Soutine never forgot that he had come to Paris to paint like the masters he idolized. In the early years he talked mainly of Tintoretto and El Greco. His enthusiasm for Rembrandt developed a little later. He professed not to like van Gogh, but it seems evident that van Gogh's late Provençal landscapes must have emboldened him in his early approach to both landscape and portraiture."[1]

"His usual practice was to complete each picture in a single working session. From the start he knew exactly what he intended, and changed his conception scarcely at all. But on a given occasion for some reason his hand might falter, his brush miscarry. The model was restless; he suffered from his indigestion; someone's ill-considered remark stuck in his mind and vexed him. Finally he would call it a day and carry the canvas up to his room and lock it in a cupboard. Then at midnight or early next morning he would take it out and pass judgement on it, and if he found it inferior, cut it up with a knife. But this did not mean discouragement or abandonment of the picture in question. Instantly he took another canvas and began all over again. Day after day he persisted like this until he had consummated his inspiration or at least assuaged it. What he aspired to, and every so often achieved, was an effect of overwhelming excitement and uninhibited force; an instantaneous vision implacably fixed."[2]

[1] Wheeler, *Soutine*, page 42 and 43. [2] *ibid*, page 79.

Collection: M. Knoedler & Co., Inc., New York; Fine Arts Associates, New York.

Chaim Soutine 1894-1943

81 LANDSCAPE AT CAGNES

Oil on canvas, 28¾ × 36¼

(1922)

Unsigned

"Soon after the strong Céret pictures, and so different in style that it is like a reversal of esthetics, comes a large view of Cagnes mainly in dark emerald and vibrant yellow, with a little mother-of-pearl house at the left. Once more all is tipped over sidewise but not this time as in an earthquake. The composition, held together with an armature of dark trees, is so strong that the earth stands firm under it. In spite of the brilliant sunshine, there is an effect of storm, of wind hissing and foliage whipping, and the walls of the hill town seem responsive to this, the rooftops belabored as by lightning strokes."[1]

"It is important to note how little room for sky is allowed in these paintings. This may be because of the oppressiveness of the over-hanging mountains. But even when it does appear, it is painted rather like foliage, and has no real vacuity or airiness."[2]

[1] Wheeler, *Soutine*, page 45. [2] *ibid*, page 65.

Collection: Paul Guillaume, Paris; Valentine Gallery, New York.

Exhibited: 23 Paintings by Soutine, Valentine Gallery, New York, March 20–April 8, 1939, number 5; *Two Russians, Soutine–Chagall*, The Institute of Contemporary Art, Boston, January 24–February 25, 1945, number 31 as "Landscapes near Cannes"; *Soutine*, The Museum of Modern Art, New York, November 1, 1950–January 7, 1951, and The Cleveland Museum of Art, January 31–March 18, 1951, page 65, catalogued page 112 and reproduced in color page 17; *Chaim Soutine*, XXVI Biennale di Venezia, June 14–October 19, 1952, page 182, number 7 as "Paesaggio a Cagnes"; *Cent Tableaux de Soutine*, Galerie Charpentier, Paris, June–October 1959, number 53 and reproduced in the catalogue.

Reference: Modigliani, Chagall, Soutine, Pascin: Some Aspects of Expressionism, by Paolo d'Ancona, Milan 1952, page 62.

81

Chaim Soutine 1894-1943

82 SIDE OF BEEF

Oil on canvas, 27½ × 20½

(1922–23)

Signed lower left, "Soutine"

"We now come to the great series of still lifes of hulking carcasses of animals, suspended fowl, and fish. In the late twenties one scarcely heard mention of Soutine without some scandalized discourse about the gruesome circumstances of their production. When he lived in *La Ruche*, he had made friends with slaughter-house employees, and practised painting pieces of meat which he got from them. About 1922, he painted an admirable *Side of Beef* in forthright realism, with the vivid red of steak, the ivory and pale gold of suet, and a finely realized hollowness inside the curved ribs."[1]

"What inspired him was the configuration of the external world, though none of the details contributory to versimilitude impressed him very much. In exuberant celebration of the natural forms, he developed upon his canvas supernatural jewel-like pigments and arbitrary rugged textures, and carried the over-all pattern so far that we scarcely know or care what it represents. But it expresses what inspired it with a force of emotion stronger than most abstract canvases."[2]

[1] Wheeler, *Soutine*, page 68. [2] *ibid*, page 50.

Collection: Valentine Gallery, New York; Mrs. Lloyd Bruce Westcott, Clinton, New Jersey.

Exhibited: Soutine, The Museum of Modern Art, New York, November 1, 1950–January 7, 1951, and The Cleveland Museum of Art, January 31–March 18, 1951, page 68, catalogued page 112 and reproduced page 68; *Soutine*, A Circulating Exhibition of The Museum of Modern Art, New York, 1951–52; *Kokoschka–Soutine*, The Arts Club of Chicago, October 1–31, 1956, number 51.

Reference: Soutine et son Temps, by Emile Szittya, Paris 1955, page 65, footnote 2.

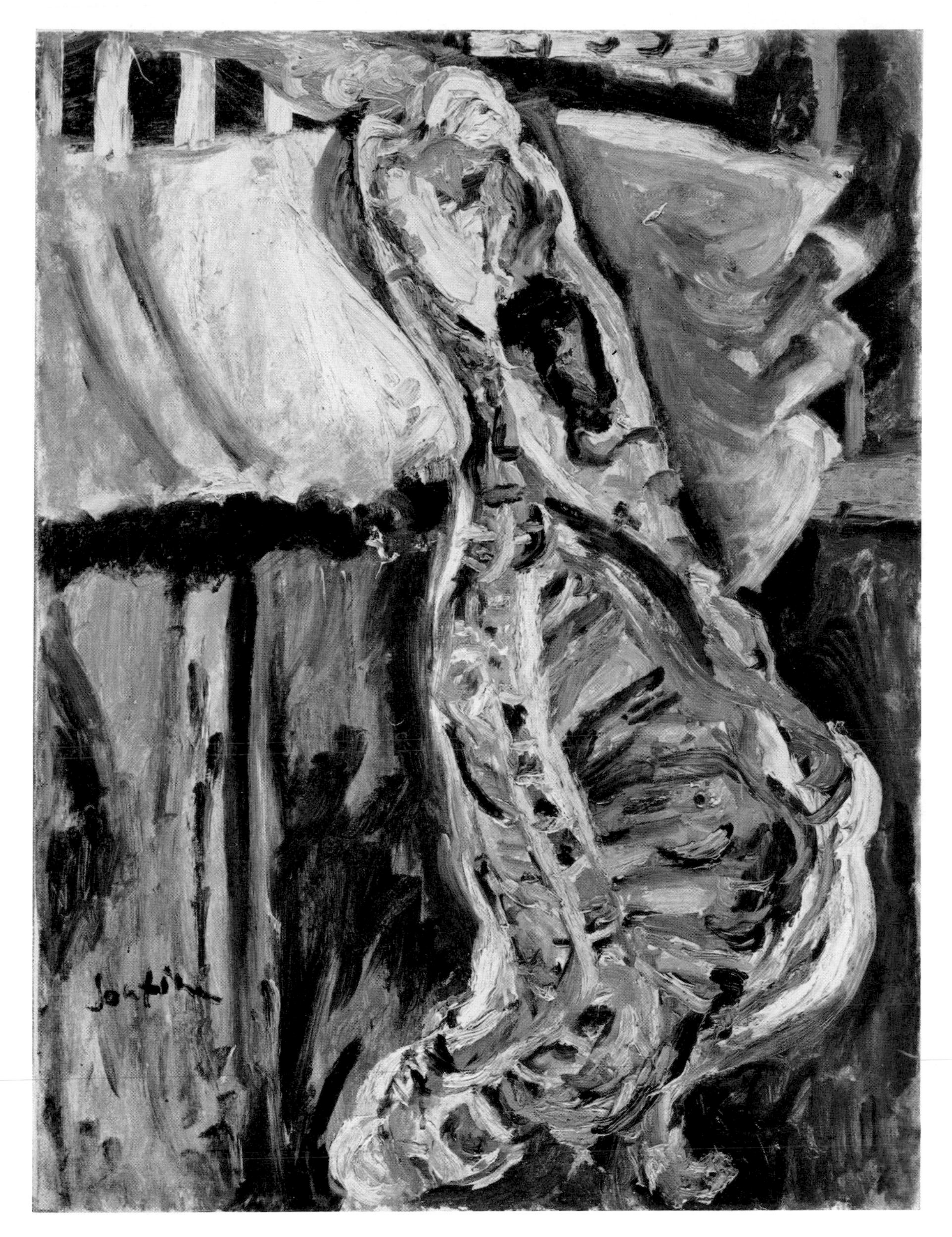

Chaim Soutine 1894-1943

83 LANDSCAPE AT VENCE

Oil on canvas, $23\frac{1}{2} \times 31\frac{3}{4}$

(1923)

Signed lower left, "C. Soutine"

". . . we observe a singularity that was to occur frequently in his work for a number of years – everything violently inclines to the right. In the great case of El Greco there was a somewhat similar trait, a twisted perpendicularity in canvas after canvas, and some critics on Spanish art have suggested that it may have derived from a disorder of eyesight. The slanting landscapes of Soutine might be explained in some such way, but if the trouble was optical, he was presently to recover from it." (Wheeler, *Soutine*, pages 46 and 48.)

Collection: Paul Guillaume, Paris; James Johnson Sweeney, New York; Valentine Gallery, New York.

Exhibited: Soutine (on the occasion of the fiftieth birthday of the artist), Niveau Gallery, New York, October 7–November 2, 1944, number 3 and dated 1922; *School of Paris*, Valentine Gallery, New York, March 25–April 13, 1946, number 20; *Group Show*, Boston Museum of Fine Arts – Museum School, Boston, March 6–20, 1950; *Works of Art Belonging to Alumnae*, Smith College Museum of Art, Northampton, Massachusetts, May–June 1950, number 76; *Summer Loan Show*, The Metropolitan Museum of Art, New York, July–August 1950; *New York Private Collections*, The Museum of Modern Art, New York, June 26–September 12, 1951.

Reference: "Rockefeller, Whitney, Senior, Odets, Colin", by Henry McBride, *Art News*, Summer 1951, page 36.

83

Chaim Soutine 1894-1943

84 WHITE HOUSE ON A HILL

Oil on canvas, $20\frac{5}{8} \times 25$

(1924)

Signed lower left, "C. Soutine"

This is the first painting acquired by the present collectors. At the time it was purchased, it seemed quite "wild" and disturbed. Today it seems almost restful and traditional. In fact, it has been referred to by a critic-friend of the collectors as their "suburban Soutine". So quickly does the public eye learn to catch up with the artist!

Collection: Valentine Gallery, New York.

Exhibited: 23 Paintings by Soutine, Valentine Gallery, New York, March 20 – April 8, 1939, number 1; *Two Russians, Soutine – Chagall*, The Institute of Contemporary Art, Boston, January 24 – February 25, 1945, number 37 as "House on a Hill".

Reference: "Soutine turns to Classicism", by Doris Brian, *Art News*, March 18, 1939, reproduced page 7 as "Paysage of 1924".

84

Chaim Soutine 1894-1943

85 LE GARCON D'ETAGE (The Floor Waiter)

Oil on canvas, 30 × 25

(1928)

Unsigned

"At the end of the twenties there followed a group of *valets-de-chambres* in scarlet vests. One moody, with a rosy-face; another astride a chair, seems ready to spring to his feet with necessary alacrity. In those years, Soutine seemed to work from color to color, the entire gamut of whites, deep blues,[1] dusky greens and, as always, back to his life-long color red. . . .

"What a boon for Soutine that the servant class in France should have kept so many archaic styles of garment, fancy dress without frivolity, which enabled him to strike that note of pitiable grandeur that was compulsive in his mind and heart, and thus avoid our modern drabness."[2]

[1] See number 86 of this catalogue. [2] Wheeler, *Soutine*, pages 73 and 74.

Collection: Henri Laurens, Paris; Nadine Effront, Paris; Max Moos, Geneva.

Exhibited: New York Private Collections, The Museum of Modern Art, New York, June 26–September 12, 1951; *Some Businessmen Collect Contemporary Art*, Dallas Museum of Fine Arts, April 6–27, 1952, number 48; *Soutine*, Museum of Art, Rhode Island School of Design, Providence, March 1953; *Soutine*, Perls Galleries, New York, November 2–December 5, 1953, number 19; *Kokoschka-Soutine*, The Arts Club of Chicago, October 1–31, 1956, number 52; *Cent Tableaux de Soutine*, Galerie Charpentier, Paris, June–October, 1959, number 43, reproduced in the catalogue and dated 1923.

85

Chaim Soutine 1894–1943

86 PORTRAIT OF A BOY IN BLUE

Oil on canvas, 30 × 23

(1929)

Signed upper right, "Soutine"

"In the early thirties, Soutine was at the peak of his career. From that point on he was entitled to all the fortune and worldwide repute that art can confer, if only he had continued to paint as diligently as in the previous decade. He had resolved and alleviated his preoccupation with painful subject matter. He had transcended all the classifications of the schools, expressionism, neo-classicism, and so forth; on the other hand his art no longer seemed very eccentric to anyone. But by his nature Soutine could not be contented or easy in mind; and in the final decade one may observe certain changes in his painting technique, with perhaps a new orientation of his enthusiasms about painters of the past. He did not live to bring all of this to fruition in any great number of canvases, but his purpose was manifested plainly enough; to become somewhat less dependent upon his genius for color, to achieve a strong mastery of his third dimension and of linear design.

"It is easy to see the gradual development of this tendency if we look first at characteristic works of the late twenties, then at his production in more or less the same category; for example, portraiture. In the *Portrait of a Boy in Blue*, a powerful, true portrait, a speaking likeness, the method of portrayal is by accumulation of tiny patches of color, one impinging on the other, close in value, seeming to fuse or melt together. There are no very marked contrasts except between the two main areas, flesh and fabric. Only some outside contours have been emphasized by deepening the recessive shadow somewhat as Cézanne did." (Wheeler, *Soutine*, pages 90 and 92.)

Collection: Madame Madeleine Castaing, Paris, from the artist; Mrs. Lloyd Bruce Wescott, Clinton, New Jersey.

Exhibited: Paintings by Haïm Soutine, The Arts Club of Chicago, December 13–30, 1935, number 20 as "Portrait of a Man"; *Soutine*, The Museum of Modern Art, New York, November 1, 1950–January 7, 1951, and The Cleveland Museum of Art, January 31–March 18, 1951, page 90, catalogued page 113 and reproduced in color page 23; *Chaim Soutine*, XXVI Biennale di Venezia, June 14–October 19, 1952, page 182, number 14 as "Ritratto di Ragazzo in blu"; *American and French Modern Masters*, Wildenstein Galleries, New York, May 4–28, 1955, number 29.

References: Modigliani, Chagall, Soutine, Pascin: Aspects of Expressionism, by Paolo d'Ancona, Milan 1952, page 66, reproduced in color page 57; *Soutine*, by Jacques Lassaigne, Paris 1954, plate 16 in color.

Chaim Soutine 1894-1943

87 FEMALE NUDE

Oil on canvas, $18\frac{1}{8} \times 10\frac{5}{8}$

1933

Signed lower right, "Soutine 1933"

"There is only one nude by Soutine, so far as we know, a small but important sketch, like a footnote to the foregoing great canvas [the Woman Bathing]. This surely was no countrywoman; probably a model, certainly not self-conscious, accustomed to the regard of men, artistic or otherwise. She has just stepped forward out of the dark of corridor or doorway, into an unflattering light; her exceptionally large eyes glitter at us. In a way it is a humorous picture, as some of Rembrandt's are; a more or less professional Susanna, with no elders visible." (Wheeler, *Soutine*, page 83.)

Collection: Mrs. Lloyd Bruce Wescott, Clinton, New Jersey who acquired it from the artist, through Madame Madeleine Castaing, in the Spring of 1934.

Exhibited: Paintings by Haïm Soutine, The Arts Club of Chicago, December 13–20, 1935, number 19; *Two Russians, Soutine – Chagall*, The Institute of Contemporary Art, Boston, January 24–February 25, 1945, number 45; *Soutine*, The Museum of Modern Art, New York, November 1, 1950–January 7, 1951, and The Cleveland Museum of Art, January 31–March 18, 1951, page 83, catalogued page 113 and reproduced page 92; *Kokoschka-Soutine*, The Arts Club of Chicago, October 1–31, 1956, number 53; *Cent Tableaux de Soutine*, Galerie Charpentier, Paris, June–October 1959, number 105 as "Nu" and reproduced in the catalogue.

87

Chaim Soutine 1894-1943

88 FISH

Oil on panel, $13\frac{3}{4} \times 30\frac{1}{2}$

(1933)

Signed lower right, "Soutine"

"This was the period when he most often borrowed subject matter for his pictures from various masterpieces of the past. But the retrospective turn of his mind in middle life was altogether different from his youthful enthusiasm, it was rather culminative than formative. Soutine's taste was never eclectic, his thought about art not at all sophisticated. In his several derivative works we do not discern any intention of parody or paradox, or of a learned esthetic synthesis. Simply seized by admiration for his two or three great men, he felt a proud desire to be classified with them. Feeling his own strength, the itch of his now matured technique, he would demonstrate what he could do with the theme and problems they had proposed.

"Courbet had painted an exceptionally large fish; and now likewise Soutine, modelling the eyes and mouth and gills of a salmon with bits of sharp relief, tapering it away in muted under-water colors. . . ."[1]

"Soutine's style bore no general relationship to Courbet's; but if one looks close, especially if one enlarges certain details, one may see what enchanted the modern painter. It was the painterliness above all, oil-painting for its own sake, with translucence and heavy texture and rugged handling. . . ."[2]

[1] Wheeler, *Soutine,* page 79. [2] *ibid,* page 81.

Collection: Lucien Lefebvre-Foinet, Paris.

Exhibited: Soutine (on the occasion of the artist's fiftieth birthday), Niveau Gallery, New York, October 7–November 2, 1944, number 7 and dated 1926; *Soutine,* The Museum of Modern Art, New York, November 1, 1950–January 7, 1951, and The Cleveland Museum of Art, January 31–March 18, 1951, page 79 as "Salmon", catalogued page 113 and reproduced page 86.

Reference: Notable Modern French and Other Paintings. Property of J. J. Puritz . . . and Other Owners, New York, January 17–18, 1945, number 149.

88

Chaim Soutine 1894-1943

89 ALLEY OF TREES

Oil on canvas, $29\frac{1}{2} \times 26\frac{1}{2}$

(1936)

Unsigned

"The last of Soutine's pictures in an important set or series were landscapes featuring trees. Tree worship is a cult anciently established in the Lithuanian part of Russia. In Soutine's youth there were still arboreal rites in villages not far removed from Smilovitchi [where he was born, near Minsk], and at the foot of any very noble specimen in the countryside one might find offerings. . . . In any case no other notable contemporary painter has offered us portraiture of so many individual trees of distinct character, with strong romantic implications.

"The *Alley of Trees* was painted at the Grand Prés near Chartres; it was a theme which he undertook several times, always effectively. Painted in extraordinarily thick impasto, as years before in Céret, apparently they are poplar trees, growing in the collective shape of a very tall arch or portal, on which the uppermost twigs and the brightness of the sky seem to ramble in delicate liveliness. The light gleams through the boughs, a mysterious little crimson cottage shines out from beyond the tree trunks, and two miniature personages somewhat grandly gesture as they proceed along the narrow road." (Wheeler, *Soutine*, pages 100, 101 and 104.)

Collection: Mrs. Lloyd Bruce Wescott, Clinton, New Jersey, from the artist, through Madame Madeleine Castaing.

Exhibited: Paintings by Haïm Soutine, The Arts Club of Chicago, December 13–30, 1935, number 18; *Soutine,* The Museum of Modern Art, New York, November 1, 1950–January 7, 1951, and The Cleveland Museum of Art, January 31–March 18, 1951, page 101, catalogued page 114 and reproduced in color page 29; *Chaim Soutine,* XXVI Biennale di Venezia, June 14–October 19, 1952, page 182, number 16 as "Viale"; *Soutine,* Museum of Art, Rhode Island School of Design, Providence, March 1953; *American and French Modern Masters,* Wildenstein Galleries, New York, May 4–28, 1955, number 30; *Paintings from Private Collections,* The Museum of Modern Art, New York, May 31–September 5, 1955; *Kokoschka–Soutine,* The Arts Club of Chicago, October 1–31, 1956, number 57; *Paintings in Alumnae Collections,* Smith College Museum of Art, Northampton, Massachusetts, October 14–November 17, 1959.

References: Town and Country, August 1946, reproduced in color as frontispiece, page 90; *Modigliani, Chagall, Soutine, Pascin: Aspects of Expressionism,* by Paolo d'Ancona, Milan 1952, page 65; *Soutine,* by Jacques Lassaigne, Paris, 1954, reproduced in color plate 13; *Soutine et son Temps,* by Emile Szittya, Paris 1955, listed in "Tableau Chronologique" page 117 as "L'Allée d'arbres"; *Arts,* November 1959, reproduced page 24.

89

Rufino Tamayo 1899-

90 PORTRAIT OF OLGA

Oil on canvas, 48 × 35

1945

Signed lower right, "Tamayo 0-45"

"Tamayo is no painter of local history, and a large part of his work makes no national reference. In a style absolutely Mexican, he achieves universal expression. His inspiration is based partly on love of country, part on love of nature. He has the ability to make himself understood by both simple folk and sophisticates – an achievement less difficult for writers than artists. Faust and Don Quixote found it easier, for example, to make their ideas clear to the common people. In painting, this is more difficult, but Tamayo – spontaneously or deliberately – has combined poetry with his painting and in thus joining the two arts he has been able to bring to the people, through his pictures, all the drama, pain, restlessness and mystery of life, expressed in moving beauty." (Enrique F. Gual, *Rufino Tamayo*, Mexico City n.d.)

Collection: Valentine Gallery, New York, from the artist.

Exhibited: Recent Tamayo Paintings, Valentine Gallery, New York, January 7–21, 1946, number 1; *Tamayo – 20 Años de su Labor Pictorica. Exposicion del Instituto Nacional de Bellas Artes*, Mexico City, Summer 1948, number 40 and reproduced in the catalogue; *Art Mexicain du Précolombien à nos Jours*, Musée National d'Art Moderne, Paris, May–June 1952, catalogued volume II, number 1073; *Mexikansk Konst fron Forntid till Nutid*, Liljevalchs Konsthall, Stockholm, September 1952, number 1058; *Exhibition of Mexican Art from Pre-Columbian Times to the Present Day*, The Tate Gallery, London, March 4–April 26, 1953, number 1050.

Reference: Rufino Tamayo, by Robert Goldwater, New York 1947, page 36 and reproduced page 103, plate LXI.

Rufino Tamayo 1899-

91 CHILDREN'S GAMES

Oil on canvas, $51\frac{1}{4} \times 76\frac{3}{4}$

1959

Signed upper right, "Tamayo '59"

The following statement of Tamayo's present feeling about artistic expression was prepared specially for this catalogue:

"Claro está que es necesario inventar lenguajes nuevos, que expresen más certeramente el concepto de la vida contemporanea, con todas sus espectaculares y casi imprevistas manifestaciones; pero me parece que es un error, contentarse tan solo con el ejercicio de ellos como única finalidad de la pintura.

"Hemos de convenie que en ella, la forma de expresión es tan solo uno de sus tantos elementos de formación, cuyo valor está en relación con los otros valores plásticos que la integran.

"Por otra parte, si la pintura utiliza un lenguaje, quiere decir que lo hace para establecer comunicación, en cuyo caso, es menester que encuentre un denominador común que lo identifique, aunque sea en mínima parte, con el espectador, si es que en realidad pretende establecer contacto con él. A mi juicio, es la naturaleza, con todas sus ilimitadas posibilidades, la que ofrece el mejor punto de encuentro entre ambos, y es a su vez el hombre, en quien se quintaesencia el milagro de ella. No cabe duda hoy, mas que en ningún otro momento, la presencia del hombre, con todo el poder de su fuerza creadora, es evidente.

"Ojalá que la pintura, tan preocupada en renovarse, no se olvide de él. R. TAMAYO"

Tamayo's statement translated by René d'Harnoncourt:

"To express adequately our acceptance of modern life with all its unforeseen developments and radical and dramatic departures from tradition, art needs a new way of expression. However, to find a new way of expression in painting is not enough. Manner of expression is one of many elements that together produce a work of art.

"Such manner in art, as in literature, is the form given to communication, and to establish communication it is essential that artist and viewer find some elements in the message that has meaning to both of them.

"I believe that nature with its unlimited variations, and man as the quintessence of nature, remains the best point of meaningful contact between artist and viewer. There is no doubt that today man with the power of his creative force should be present in modern art.

"Let us hope that painting in its search for new forms will not forget man.

R. TAMAYO"

Collection: From the artist, Paris, May 1959.

Exhibited: Tamayo, The Knoedler Gallery, New York, November 17–December 12, 1959, number 24.

91

Jean Dubuffet 1901-

92 MOULEUSE DE CAFE (The Coffee-Grinder)

Oil, sand and other materials on canvas, $45\frac{1}{2} \times 35$

1945

Signed on the back, "J. Dubuffet Noël 1945"

Excerpts from Jean Dubuffet's notes for a lecture on "Anticultural Positions", delivered at The Arts Club of Chicago, December 20, 1951:

"I think, not only in the arts, but also in many other fields, an important change is taking place, now, in our time, in the frame of mind of many persons.

"It seems to me that certain values, which had been considered for a long time as very certain and beyond discussion, begin now to appear doubtful, and even quite false, to many persons. And that, on the other hand, other values, which were neglected, or held in contempt, or even quite unknown, begin to appear of great worth.

"I have the impression that a complete liquidation of all the ways of thinking, whose sum constituted what has been called humanism and has been fundamental for our culture since the Renaissance, is now taking place, or, at least, going to take place soon.

"I think the increasing knowledge of the thinking of so-called primitive peoples, during the past fifty years, has contributed a great deal to this change, and especially the acquaintance with works of art made by these peoples, which have much surprised and interested the occidental public.

"It seems to me that especially many persons begin to ask themselves if Occident has not many very important things to learn from these savages. May be, in many cases, their solutions and their ways of doing, which first appeared to us very rough, are more clever than ours. It may be ours are the rough ones. It may be refinement, cerebrations, depth of mind, are on their side, and not on ours." (*Continued in the text of number 93.*)

Collection: Pierre Matisse Gallery, New York, from the artist.

Exhibited: J. Dubuffet Paintings, Pierre Matisse Gallery, New York, January 7–February 1, 1947, number 14; *Paintings by Jean Dubuffet,* Pierre Matisse Gallery, New York, January–February 1950, number 8.

References: Mirobolus Macadam & Cie, Hautespates de J. Dubuffet, by Michel Tapié, Paris 1946, mentioned page 35 as "Cafetière", reproduced page 9; *Prospectus aux Amateurs de Tout Genre,* by Jean Dubuffet, Paris 1946, page 9 *et seq*; *Look,* May 9, 1950, reproduced page 35; *Tableau Bon Levain à Vous de Cuire la Pate – L'Art Brut de Jean Dubuffet,* by Georges Limbour, Paris and New York 1953, reproduced page 23.

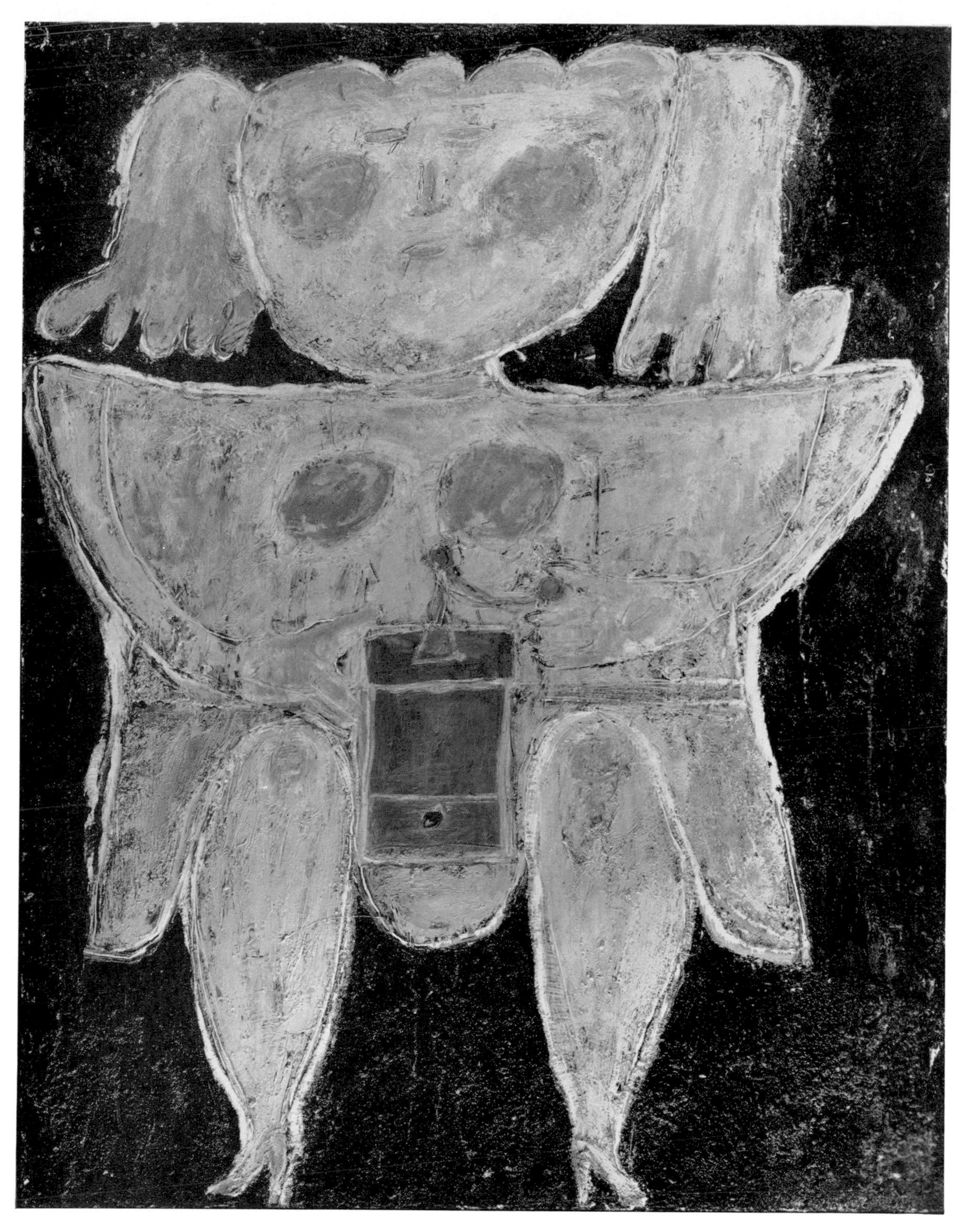

92

Jean Dubuffet 1901–

93 GRANDE VUE DE PARIS

Oil on canvas, $59\frac{1}{2} \times 79\frac{1}{2}$

1946

Signed on the back, "J. Dubuffet Millet 1946"

Excerpts from Jean Dubuffet's notes for a lecture, continued:

"Personally, I believe very much in values of savagery; I mean: instinct, passion, mood violence, madness.

"Now I must say I don't mean to say the Occident lacks these savage values. On the contrary! But I think that the values held up by our culture don't correspond to the real frame of mind of Occident. I think that the culture of Occident is a coat which does not fit him; which, in any case, doesn't fit him any more. I think this culture is very much like a dead language, without anything in common with the language spoken in the street. It is confined to certain small and dead circles, as a culture of mandarins. It no longer has real and living roots.

"For myself, I aim for an art which would be in immediate connection with daily life, an art which would start from this daily life and which would be a very direct and very sincere expression of our real life and our real moods.

"I am going to enumerate several points, concerning the occidental culture, with which I don't agree.

"One of the principal characteristics of Western culture is the belief that the nature of man is very different from the nature of other beings of the world . . . On the contrary, the so-called primitive man loves and admires trees and rivers, and has a great pleasure to be like them. He believes in a real similitude between man and trees and rivers . . . [he has] a feeling that the man is not the owner of the beings, but only one of them among the others.

"My second point of disagreement with occidental culture is [that] Western man believes that the things he thinks exist outside exactly in the same way he thinks of them. He is convinced that the shape of the world is the same shape as his reason. He believes very strongly the basis of his reason is well founded, and especially the basis of his logic.

"But the primitive man has rather an idea of weakness of reason and logic, and believes rather in other ways of getting knowledge of things. That is why he has so much esteem and so much admiration for the states of mind which we call madness. I must declare I have a great interest for madness; and I am convinced art has much to do with madness." (*Continued in the text of number 94.*)

Collection: Pierre Matisse Gallery, New York, from the artist.

Exhibited: Paintings by Jean Dubuffet, Pierre Matisse Gallery, New York, January 1950, number 13; *Jean Dubuffet Retrospective Exhibition 1943–1949,* Pierre Matisse Gallery, New York, November 10–December 12, 1959, number 16a as "Façades d'immeubles", reproduced in the catalogue.

Reference: "Jean Dubuffet Paints for Pity's Sake", by Belle Krasne, *The Art Digest,* February 15, 1950, reproduced page 17.

93

Jean Dubuffet 1901-

94 HISTOIRES NATURELLES

Oil and composition on canvas, 57 × 45

1951

Signed on the back, "J. Dubuffet '51"

Excerpts from Jean Dubuffet's notes for a lecture, continued:

"Now, third point . . . The whole art, the whole literature and the whole philosophy of Occident, rest on the landing of elaborated ideas. But my own art, and my own philosophy, lean entirely on stages more underground. I try always to catch the mental process at the deeper point of its roots, where, I am sure, the sap is much richer.

"Now, fourth. Occidental culture is very fond of analysis, and I have no taste for analysis, and no confidence in it. One thinks everything can be known by way of dismantling it or dissecting it into all its parts, and studying separately each of these parts.

"My own feeling is quite different. I am more disposed, on the contrary, to always recompose things. As soon as an object has been cut only into two parts, I have the impression it is lost for my study, I am further removed from this object instead of being nearer to it . . .

"If there is a tree in the country, I don't bring it into my laboratory to look at it under my microscope, because I think the wind which blows through its leaves is absolutely necessary for the knowledge of the tree and cannot be separated from it. Also the birds which are in the branches, and even the song of these birds. My turn of mind is to join always more things which surround the tree . . . I think this turn of mind is an important factor of the aspect of my art." (*Continued in the text of number 95.*)

Collection: Pierre Matisse Gallery, New York, from the artist.

Exhibited: Landscaped Tables, Landscapes of the Mind, Stones of Philosophy, Exhibition of Paintings executed in 1950 and 1951 by Jean Dubuffet, Pierre Matisse Gallery, New York, February 12–March 1, 1952, number 7, reproduced in the catalogue.

Reference: Tableau Bon Levain à Vous de Cuire la Pate – L'Art Brut de Jean Dubuffet, by Georges Limbour, Paris and New York 1953, reproduced page 87 as "Table aux Pièces d'Histoires Naturelle".

Jean Dubuffet 1901–

95 TETE AU TEINT DE SUCRE (Head with Sugar Complexion)

Oil and composition on masonite board, 21¾ × 18

1951

Signed lower right, "J. Dubuffet 51"

Excerpts from Jean Dubuffet's notes for a lecture, continued:

"The fifth point, now, is that our culture is based on an enormous confidence in the language – and especially the written language; and belief in its ability to translate and elaborate thought. That appears to me a misapprehension. I have the impression language is a rough, very rough stenography, a system of algebraic signs very rudimentary, which impairs thought instead of helping it . . .

"I believe (and here I am in accord with the so-called primitive civilizations) that painting is more concrete than the written words, and is a much more rich instrument for the expression and elaboration of thought.

"I have just said, what interests me in thought, is not the instant of transformation into formal ideas, but the moments preceding that. My painting can be regarded as a tentative language fitting for these areas of thought.

"I come to my sixth and last point, and I intend now to speak of the notion of beauty adopted by occidental culture.

"I want to begin by telling you in which my own conception of the notion of beauty differs from the usual one.

"The latter believes that there are beautiful objects and ugly objects, beautiful persons and ugly persons, beautiful places and ugly places, and so forth.

"Not I. I believe beauty is nowhere. I consider this notion of beauty as completely false. I refuse absolutely to assent to this idea . . . I think the Greeks are the ones, first, to purport that certain objects are more beautiful than others.

"The so-called savage nations don't believe in that at all. They don't understand when you speak to them of beauty. This is the reason one calls them savage. The Western man gives the name of savage to one who doesn't understand that beautiful things and ugly things exist, and who doesn't care for that at all." (*Continued in the text of number 96.*)

Collection: Pierre Matisse Gallery, New York, from the artist.

Exhibited: Landscaped Tables, Landscapes of the Mind, Stones of Philosophy, Exhibition of Paintings executed in 1950 and 1951 by Jean Dubuffet, Pierre Matisse Gallery, New York, February 12–March 1, 1952, number 14.

Reference: "New York Report," by Martica Sawin, *Art International*, volume III/10, 1959–60, reproduced page 52.

95

Jean Dubuffet 1901-

96 TETE AU NEZ LILAS (Head with Lilac Nose)

Oil and composition on masonite board, 32 × 25½

1951

Signed lower right, "J. Dubuffet 51"

Excerpts from Jean Dubuffet's notes for a lecture, continued:

"What is strange is that, for centuries and centuries, and still now more than ever, the men of occident dispute which are the beautiful things and which are the ugly ones. All are certain that beauty exists without doubt, but one cannot find two who agree about the objects which are endowed. And from one century to the next it changes. The occidental culture declares beautiful, in each century, what it declared ugly in the preceding one . . .

"This idea of beauty is however one of the things our culture prizes most, and it is customary to consider this belief in beauty, and the respect for this beauty, as the ultimate justification of Western civilization, and the principle of civilization itself is involved with this notion of beauty.

"I find this idea of beauty a meager and not very ingenious invention, and especially not very encouraging for man. It is distressing to think about people deprived of beauty because they have not a straight nose, or are too corpulent, or too old. I find even this idea that the world we live in is made up of ninety percent ugly things and ugly places, while things and places endowed with beauty are very rare and difficult to meet. I must say, I find this idea not very exciting. It seems to me that the Western man will not suffer a great loss if it loses this idea. On the contrary, if he becomes aware that there is no ugly object nor ugly person in the world, and that any object of the world is able to become for any man a way of fascination and illumination, he will have made a very good catch. I think such an idea will enrich life more than the Greek idea of beauty." (*Continued in the text of number 97.*)

Collection: Pierre Matisse Gallery, New York, from the artist.

Exhibited: Landscaped Tables, Landscapes of the Mind, Stones of Philosophy, Exhibition of Paintings executed in 1950 and 1951 by Jean Dubuffet, Pierre Matisse Gallery, New York, February 12–March 1, 1952, number 5; *The Embellished Surface*, Circulating Exhibition of The Museum of Modern Art, New York, 1953–54.

References: Time, March 3, 1952, reproduced page 60; "The Year's Best: 1952", *Art News*, January 1953, reproduced page 43; "Jean Dubuffet", by John Anthony Thwaites, *Arts Yearbook 3*, 1959, reproduced page 133.

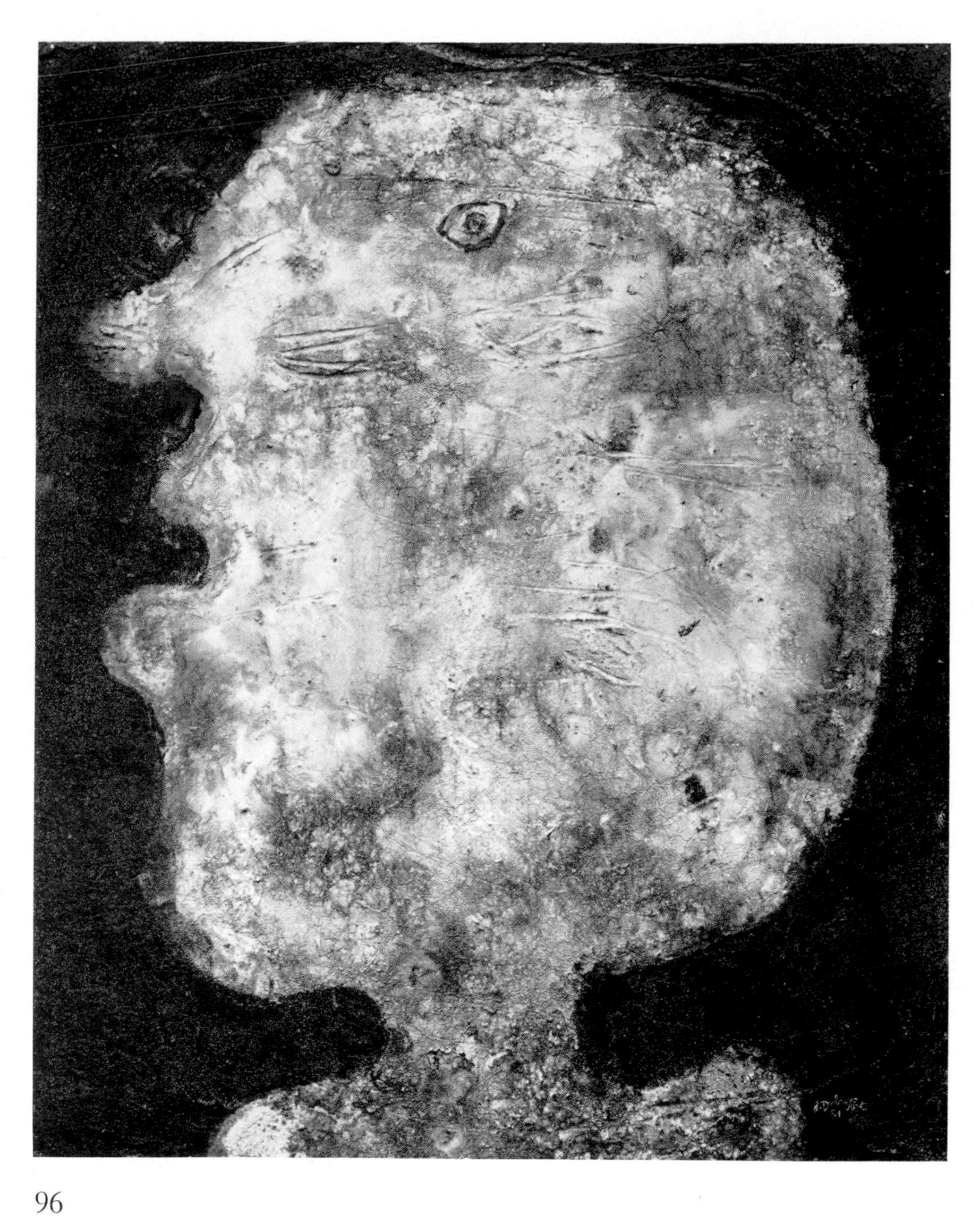

96

Jean Dubuffet 1901-

97 LA MONTAGNE ROSE (The Rose Mountain)

Oil and composition on masonite board, 36 × 48

1952

Signed lower center, "J. Dubuffet 52"

Excerpts from Jean Dubuffet's notes for a lecture, continued:

"And now what happens with art? Art has been considered, since the Greeks, to have as its goal the creation of beautiful lines and beautiful color harmonies. If one abolishes this notion, what becomes of art? I am going to tell you. Art then returns to its real function, much more significant than creating shapes and colors agreeable from a so-called pleasure of the eyes.

"I don't find this function, assembling colors in pleasing arrangements, very noble. If painting was only that, I should not lose one hour of my time in this activity. Art addresses itself to the mind, and not to the eyes. It has always been considered in this way by primitive peoples, and they are right. Art is a language, instrument of knowledge, instrument of expression . . .

". . . painting is, in my opinion a language richer than that of words. So it is quite useless to look for rationalizations in art. Painting is a language much more immediate, and, at the same time, much more charged with meaning. Painting operates through signs which are not abstract and incorporeal like words. The signs of painting are much closer to the objects themselves. Further, painting manipulates materials which are themselves living substances. That is why painting allows one to go much further than words do, in approaching things and conjuring them. (*Continued in the text of number 98.*)

Collection: Pierre Matisse Gallery, New York, from the artist.

Exhibited: Landscaped Tables, Landscapes of the Mind, Stones of Philosophy, Exhibition of Paintings executed in 1950 and 1951 by Jean Dubuffet, Pierre Matisse Gallery, New York, February 12–March 1, 1952, number 9.

97

Jean Dubuffet 1901-

98 VACHE A L'HERBAGE (Cow in Pasture)

Oil on canvas, 38 × 45

1954

Signed upper right, "J. Dubuffet 54"

Excerpts from Jean Dubuffet's notes for a lecture, concluded:

"Painting has a double advantage over language of words. First, painting conjures objects with greater strength, and comes closer to them. Second, painting opens, to the inner dance of the painter's mind, a larger door to the outside. These two qualities of painting make it an extraordinary instrument of thought, or, if you will, an extraordinary instrument of clairvoyance, and also an extraordinary instrument to exteriorize their clairvoyance, and to permit us to get it ourselves also with the painter.

"Painting now, using these two powerful means, can illuminate the world with wonderful discoveries, can endow man with new myths, and new mystics, and reveal, in infinite number, unsuspected aspects of things, and new values not yet perceived.

"Here is, I think, for artists, a much more worthy job than creating assemblages of shapes and colors pleasing for the eyes."

Collection: Pierre Matisse Gallery, New York, from the artist.

Exhibited: J. Dubuffet. Recent Paintings, Collages & Drawings, Pierre Matisse Gallery, New York, November 23–December 31, 1954, number 12; *The 1955 Pittsburgh International Exhibition of Contemporary Painting,* Carnegie Institute, Pittsburgh, October 13–December 18, 1955, number 82 as "Purple Cow", plate 26.

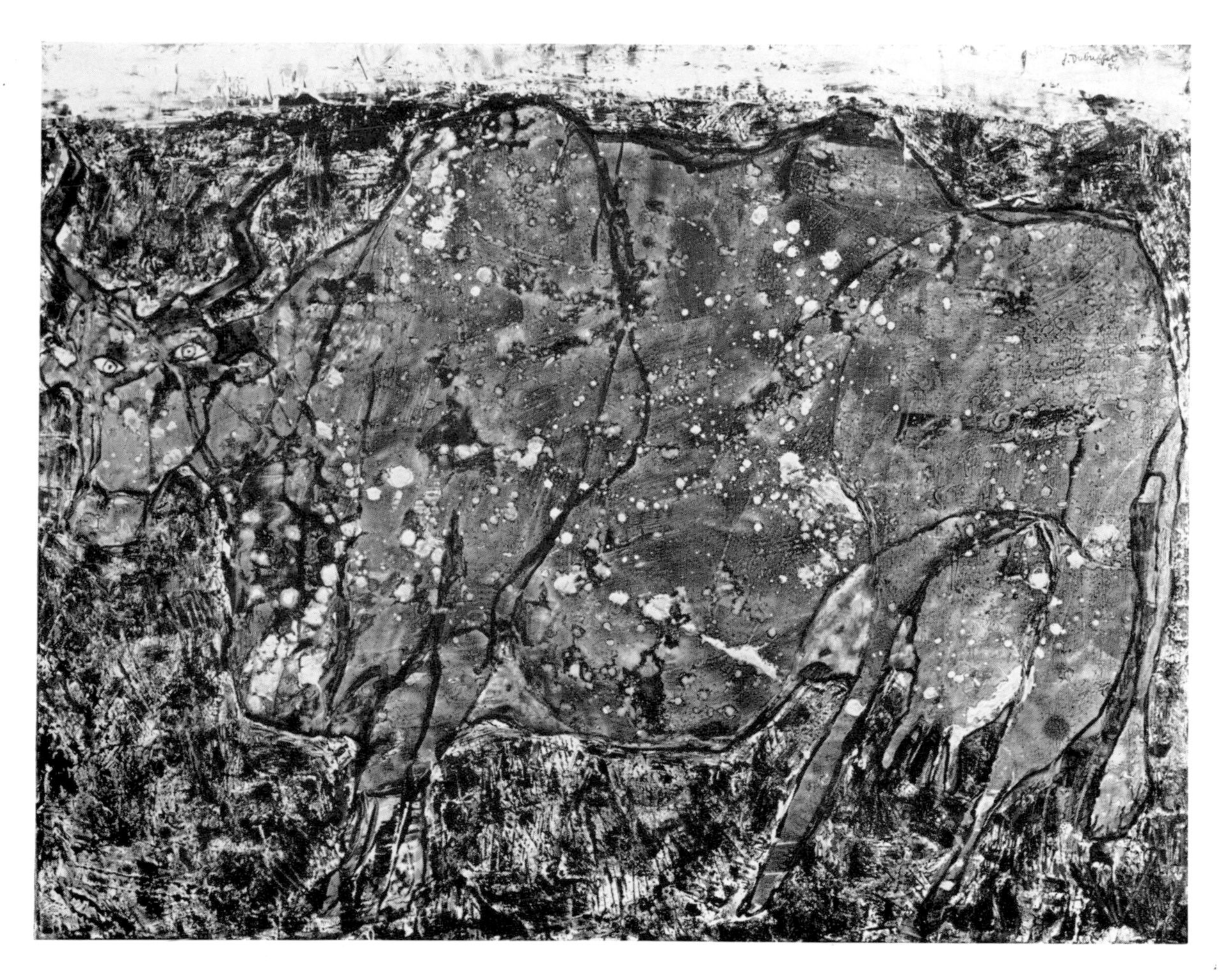

98

Jean Dubuffet 1901–

99 FEMME A LA FOURRURE (Woman with Furs)

Oil on canvas, 39½ × 32

1954

Signed upper left, "J. Dubuffet 54"

"Dubuffet's painting can be seen as an adventurous exploration of the domain of matter – a domain which until now has only been glanced at. Dubuffet's chief quality is an impetuous and *démiurgique* imagination concerning matter. But we must remember that, in its most humble elements, matter contains the primeval mud, and in its richest jewels, the secrets of the spirit. After the prelude of his first paintings [in exuberantly coloured oils], he suddenly turned to tar, asphalt, and white lead, all kneaded in thick layers on which he carved summary effigies of personages – his first idols. [These paintings on *plaques de staff* weigh almost two stone.] His matter evolved very quickly, as if it flowed from a volcano with diverse chemical and mineral resources. It was enriched with cement, plaster and many other products which it would be in vain to enumerate here, for they changed frequently and were worked with different instruments progressively as this adventure – not unlike the geological formation of our planet – proceeded." (Georges Limbour, Introduction to catalogue of the Jean Dubuffet Exhibition, Arthur Tooth & Sons, London, 1958.)

Collection: Pierre Matisse Gallery, New York, from the artist.

Exhibited: J. Dubuffet. Recent Paintings, Collages & Drawings, Pierre Matisse Gallery, New York, November 23–December 31, 1954, number 10; *New Images of Man*, The Museum of Modern Art, New York, September 28–November 29, 1959 and The Baltimore Museum of Art, January 9–February 7, 1960, number 41, reproduced page 66.

Reference: Jean Dubuffet, by James Fitzsimmons, Brussels 1958, reproduced number 51.

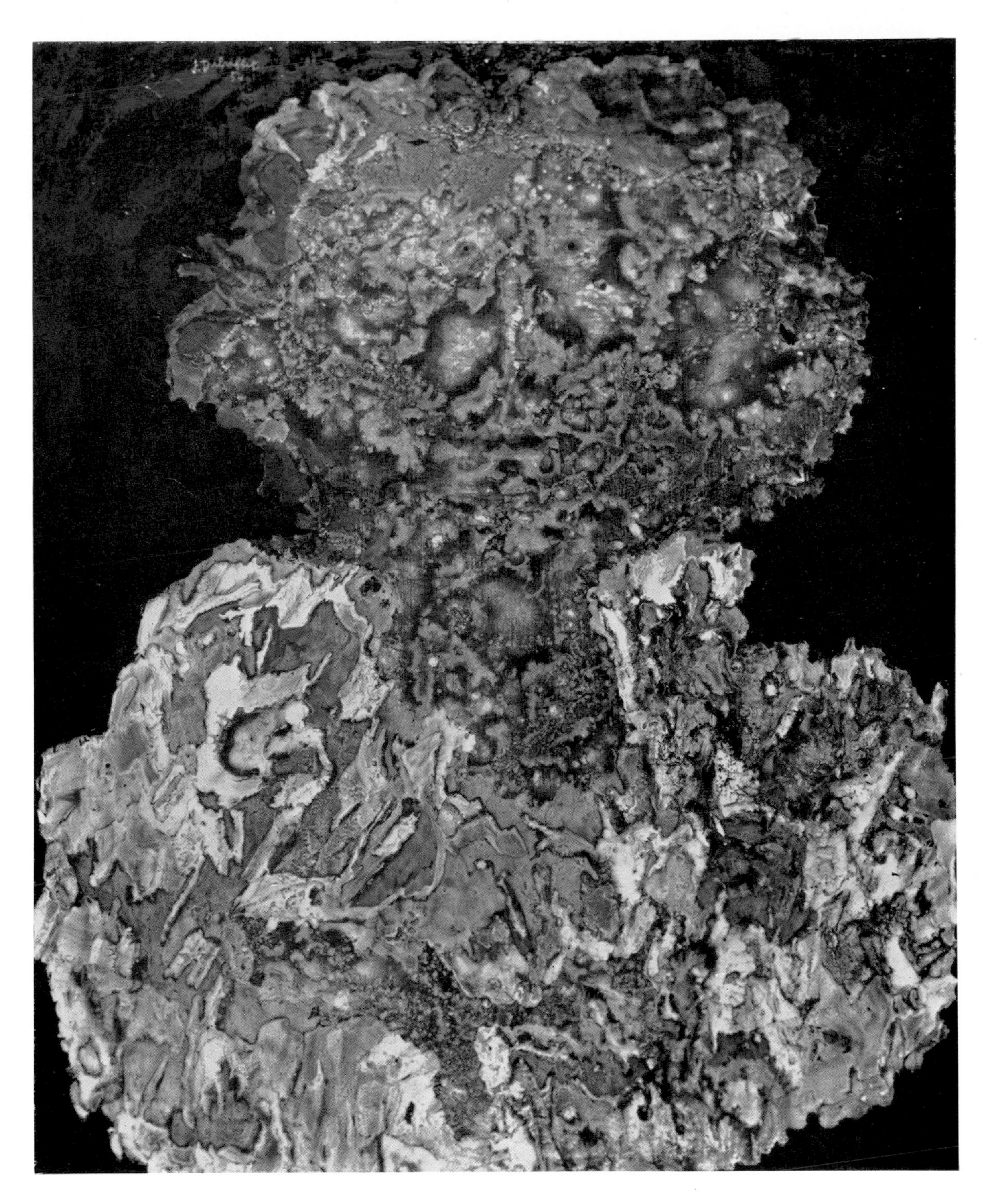

99

Jean Dubuffet 1901-

100 AFRICAN LANDSCAPE

Watercolor on paper, 8 × 10

1949

Signed lower left, "J. Dubuffet 49"

"The various landscapes set loose in the spectator the same mechanism of thought or evocation whether they are in high relief or of a smoother surface. We recognize in them no definable object, no individual rock or tree; the human silhouettes that we can perceive are made of the same matter as the rocks . . .

"Another way he likes to provoke our imagination is by confusing and mixing up scale; that is, the dimensions of the objects he represents remain extremely uncertain. In his landscapes, most of the time it is hard to say whether the picture represents a whole continent, a mountain, a cliff, or only a very small bit of ground . . ." (Georges Limbour, Introduction to catalogue of the Jean Dubuffet Exhibition, Arthur Tooth & Sons, London, 1958.)

Collection: Pierre Matisse Gallery, New York, from the artist.

100

Fritz Winter 1905-

101 MIT GELB (With Yellow)

Oil on paper, $29\frac{3}{4} \times 39\frac{1}{2}$

1954

Signed lower left, "Winter 54"

"Fritz Winter (born 1905) most clearly belongs to that fine continuity of German romantic thought that the Blaue Reiter introduced into modern sensibility and that was further developed by Klee's work. Winter started from that point. He himself went through the Bauhaus, was Kandinsky's assistant, and was in close relationship to Klee. There was in addition his own personal experience. In his youth Winter had worked as a miner and there, in the gray glimmer of the rocks, had seen and lived with sunken primeval forms, the imprints of an earlier world. . . . Faced by (his) pictures, our concepts of objective and abstract break down. We see in them, it is true, non-representational diagrams of physical and psychic energies, structures, fields of force, basic crystalline patterns. But these abstract schemes are permeated by the suggestion of a deeper connection between Winter's personal expressive world and the motivating forces of a living, organic nature, the universal in us and around us." (Werner Haftmann in *German Art of the Twentieth Century*, by Werner Haftmann, Alfred Hentzen, William S. Lieberman, edited by Andrew Carnduff Ritchie, New York 1957, page 136.)

Collection: Curt Valentin Gallery, New York, from the artist.

102 LINEAR BLAU (Linear Blue)

Oil on paper, $29\frac{3}{4} \times 39\frac{1}{2}$

1954

Signed lower right, "Winter 54"

Collection: Curt Valentin Gallery, New York, from the artist.

101

102

Morris Graves 1910–

103 WOODPECKER

Gouache on paper, 26¾ × 19¾

(1940)

Unsigned

"Graves, on the other hand, is by comparison [with Klee] single-minded and single-visioned, and we nearly always feel in him the sway of a continuous, dark mood, not lacking in humor, but too brooding for wit. This, of course, is his strength, as Klee's faceted sensitivity was his. And in his absorption in nature, Graves may more rewardingly be compared to another modern American artist, Charles Burchfield, whose early watercolors, as I have said, are among the high points of native romantic art. But there is this difference to be noted: while Burchfield recorded the preternaturalism imagined by a susceptible child, Graves lets nature's tensions play out all within nature itself – the bird against the forest silence, the giddy snake against the moon." (James Thrall Soby, *Contemporary Painters*, New York 1948, page 44).

Collection: Frank Crowninshield, New York.

Exhibited: Some Paintings from Alumnae Collections, Smith College Museum of Art, Northampton, Massachusetts, June 1948; *Contemporaty Art Collected by American Business*, MetaMold Aluminium Company, Cedarburg, Wisconsin, April 1953, number 17; *Art Our Children Live With*, The Downtown Gallery, New York, December 9–21, 1957, number 17.

Pierre Soulages 1919-

104 PAINTING 6 MARCH 55

Oil on canvas, 51 × 35

1955

Signed on the back, "Soulages 6-3-55"

"Soberness, intensity, majesty: it is even more by these three words that Soulages' art is so defined; for his also is 'Romanesque' and its nervous solemnity evokes that of the Conques church (the painter's spiritual homeland) where balance is born of the neutralization one by the other of opposed forces. There is little color in his work, but it has depth and it is dense enough to conciliate transparency and saturation. On a uniform background, bluish, greenish or brown, but one that is varied by the half-light, the form-signs detach themselves in bottle green, Prussian blue, in ochres, and especially in sumptuous blacks, velvety and hard, strong and profound, amply colored in a single tone, diversified and enriched by a thousand precious nuances: we immediately think of a ball of porphyry or onyx. This painting possesses also the tight grain quality of porphyry and onyx. The largeness of the treatment, the decision of each brush stroke takes nothing away from it; on the contrary, they add to the richness of the paint quality, full, compact, without ever achieving a quality of heaviness." (Bernard Dorival, *Twentieth Century Painters*, volume 2, New York 1958, pages 122 and 123.)

Collection: Samuel M. Kootz Gallery, New York, from the artist.

Exhibited: New Paintings by Pierre Soulages, Samuel M. Kootz Gallery, New York, May 9–28, 1955; *Soulages*, Galerie de France, Paris, March 13–April 9, 1956, number 11.

104

Jean-Paul Riopelle 1923-

105 DERIVE

Oil on canvas, 51 × 64

1952

Signed lower right, "Riopelle 52"

"Like a trapper fresh from the Canadian solitudes measuring his stride to our narrow pavements, Jean-Paul Riopelle seems hardly to contain the flooding energies of youth at its full, its impetuosity and pre-emptoriness that bid defiance to distance and bulk. His manner recalls Victor Hugo's lines:

'He so pores on Nature
That Nature has disappeared'

– to reappear suddenly as soon as he takes up his brush, so that his paintings resemble something we cannot define, all things taken together rather than any particular thing. He rejects detachment, that fruit of the intellect. His painting is purely physical, or better (not to overstate the distinction), instinctive. . . .

"It would be a mistake however to think that there is nothing left but automatism. The substructure of a purely intuitive being is no less rigorously defined than others. Its form is indefinite but not infinite. The brush-stroke applied in one corner of the canvas echoes instantaneously at the other extremity, not seen, but sensed. To accuse this painting of automatism is to reproach it with not being alive. . . ." (Georges Duthuit in the introduction [translated by Samuel Beckett] to the catalogue of the Riopelle exhibition, Matisse Gallery, New York 1954.)

Collection: Pierre Matisse Gallery, New York, from the artist.

Exhibited: Riopelle – First American Exhibition, Pierre Matisse Gallery, New York, January 5–23, 1954, number 5.

105

Jean-Paul Riopelle 1923-

106 BRUMAIRE

Oil on canvas, 45½ × 35

1953

Signed lower left, "Riopelle 53"

" 'Where can this possibly lead to? What is its future?' Irresistably the question arose, proving that this work is the image of an incipience. . . .

". . . To insist on its evolving in our direction is tantamount to having to condemn it, if it does not. Let us not be blinded by a hypothetical future to a very real present. And a very rare and choice present it is indeed, this painting which sheds the gentle splendours of its fires on the scene where we languish, frigid as an operating-theatre, and livid with the ignoble glares of publicity. For it is perhaps time to say, since painting is our theme, that the principal quality of Riopelle's pictures is their combination of extreme opulence and perfect discretion, so that our indigence is not overwhelmed by an excessive and brutal display of riches: a conflagration that is like a caress, a suave and gracious onrush of springtide." (Georges Duthuit in the introduction [translated by Samuel Beckett] to the catalogue of the Riopelle exhibition, Matisse Gallery, New York 1954.)

Collection: Pierre Matisse Gallery, New York, from the artist.

Exhibited: Riopelle – First American Exhibition, Pierre Matisse Gallery, New York, January 5–23, 1954, number 11.

Three Chinese Sculptures

107 A. PAIR OF TOMB TILES

Stone, 12¾ × 7 inches each

Han Period, 206 B.C.–A.D. 220

"All the Han Dynasty sculpture that has survived is, with few exceptions, associated with burials and tomb construction. . . .

"Although the Han stone reliefs from offering chambers are frequently described as sculpture, very few have any plastic quality, and even those rendered in low relief with slightly rounded contours and strong inner markings are essentially pictorial. . . ."[1]

The high relief and sculptural quality of these tiles is extremely rare.

[1] Laurence Sickman and Alexander Soper, *The Art and Architecture of China*, London 1956, pages 25 and 26.

Collection: C. T. Loo, New York.

107 B. PAIR OF HEADS FROM TOMB FIGURES

Clay, height 5½ and 6 inches

Han Period, 206 B.C.–A.D. 220

"Above all, the modeller in clay has left us, in the form of the figurines that accompanied the dead into the tomb, some of the best sculptures, on a reduced scale, to come out of Asia . . . the reader should know that much of the real flavour of Chinese life in the centuries from the Han to the end of the T'ang Dynasty can be recaptured to a gratifying extent through a study of the tomb figures." (Laurence Sickman and Alexander Soper, *The Art and Architecture of China*, London 1956, page 27.)

Collection: C. T. Loo, New York.

107 C. STANDING WARRIOR

Terra cotta with traces of polychrome pigments, height 16 inches

T'ang Period, A.D. 618–906

"Chinese sculpture in the round was made successfully for the first time in the T'ang Dynasty, and particularly in the eighth century. Earlier free-standing figures are essentially conceived to be viewed from the front. While most T'ang sculpture is more effective when looked at in the same way, the planes are continuous, without abrupt transitions, and the figures are statues in the true sense. This meant, of course, a break with the ancient Chinese devotion to an essentially linear style; . . ." (Laurence Sickman and Alexander Soper, *The Art and Architecture of China*, London 1956, page 73.)

Collection: C. T. Loo, New York.

107 A

107 B

107 C

Three Archaic Sculptures

108 A. AFRICAN *Bakota-Gabon (French Equatorial Africa)*

FUNERARY DOUBLE-FACE FIGURE

Wood covered with brass and copper, height 25 inches

"In some a human face is centered, sometimes with protruding forehead, convex brow indicating male, concave brow, female. Abstract ornament surrounds the head; lozenge-shaped body. Some have two faces, front and back. According to one theory, the round forms have a solar symbolism; according to another, they represent the radiation of the dead man's spirit. The body is merely indicated because after death it no longer exists." (Ladislas Segy, *African Sculpture Speaks*, New York 1952, page 186.)

Collection: Valentine Gallery, New York.

Exhibited: Summer Loan Show, The Metropolitan Museum of Art, New York, July–August 1950.

108 B. MEXICAN *Colima (Western Mexico)*

DOG – MEXICAN HAIRLESS OR *TECHICHI*

(1200–1500)

Polished red clay, height 9 inches, length 13½ inches

"The western Mexican tradition of freehand clay-modeling had its ablest and most creative artists in Colima, to the west and south of the volcano of the same name . . . The Colima potters were fine craftsmen and extraordinary artists . . .

"Best known among the clay sculptures of Colima are the life-size hollow effigies of dogs of polished red or black clay – not ordinary dogs but a peculiar species of Mexican hairless, the *techichi* or *tepescuintli*, extremely rare today but bred and fattened in pre-Spanish times especially to be eaten. The *techichi* look like inflated dachshunds with round heads and bulging eyes, upright large ears, and short bow-legs . . ." Miguel Covarrubias, *Indian Art of Mexico and Central America*, New York 1957, pages 92 and 93).

Collection: Mathias Komor, New York.

Reference: "The Laughing Lunch", by Michael Ayrton, *Vogue*, September 15, 1959, page 110 and reproduced.

108 C. JAPANESE *Haniwa*

FIGURE OF A WARRIOR

(A.D. 200–600)

Hollow clay, height 13⅞ inches

"Clay reliefs of various types can be uncovered from old places of inhabitation and burial spots in all parts of Japan . . .

"These clay remains can be classified in general as follows: Jomon Earthenwares, Dogu (clay figurines), Yayoi Earthenwares and the Haniwa. They make their appearance in that order . . .

"The Haniwa are the clay relics . . . uncovered

108 A

108 B

from the immense tombs of prosperous grandee families of the 3rd to 6th centuries . . ." (Noma Seiroku, *The Art of Clay*, Tokyo 1954, pages 1 and 8.)

There are many explanations given for their existence. One of them is that the custom of immolation [living burial of attendants to follow the dead] came to be considered tragic and that clay figures were used to replace the attendants.

Collection: Mathias Komor, New York.

108 C

Honoré Daumier 1808-1879

109 THREE BUSTS

Bronzes

(1830–32)

"Honoré Daumier's work as a sculptor is beginning to attract increased attention for its vital importance in the evolution of present-day sculpture. Through him the baroque tradition descends directly to Rodin. *Ratapoil*, 1850; the Caricature of Napoleon III; the Self-Portrait, 1855; and 36 clay busts of French deputies (Le Ventre Législatif), 1830–32, are the most outstanding examples of his manner. These busts were modeled from memory, not from life. Their most striking characteristics, like those of *Ratapoil*, are the fleeting quality of the poses, the freedom of the contours, and the intense quality of life which radiates from them. The material seems to have liquefied under the pressure of the physical and emotional atmosphere. These are more than rapid caricatures; they are prototypes of the great human comedy." (Carola Giedion-Welcker, *Contemporary Sculpture*, New York 1955, page 2.)

A. LE NIAIS (The Simpleton)

Bronze, height 5 inches

Unsigned, stamped at the back, "MLG" *and* "23/30"

Collection: Carstairs Gallery, New York.

References: Trente-six Bustes de H. Daumier, by Eugène Bouvy, Paris 1932, plate 20 from the original clay; "Bustes & Personages", by Charles Mourre, *Arts et Livres de Provence, Number 8*, Marseille 1948, page 98. Mourre disputes the suggestion that the subject may have been Girod de l'Ain, saying: "This is certainly not Girod de l'Ain, as some people have thought. So much the better, or so much the worse for Girod de l'Ain" (translation); *Daumier Sculpteur*, by Maurice Gobin, Paris 1952, catalogued number 20 as "Le Niais – (Amiral Verhuel ou Girod de l'Ain) (?)", reproduced pages 204 and 205 from the original clay.

B. L'INFATUE DE SOI (The Conceited One)

Bronze, height 6⅝ inches

Unsigned, stamped at the back, "MLG" *and* "23/25"

Collection: Carstairs Gallery, New York.

References: Trente-six Bustes de H. Daumier, by Eugène Bouvy, Paris 1932, plate 22 from the original clay; "Bustes & Personages", by Charles Mourre, *Arts et Livres de Provence, Number 8*, Marseille 1948, page 99; *Daumier Sculpteur*, by Maurice Gobin, Paris 1952, catalogued number 22 as "L'Infatué de soi – Bailliot", reproduced page 209 from the original clay.

C. UN MALIN (A Malicious One)

Bronze, height 9 inches

Unsigned, stamped at the back, "MLG" *and* "23/25"

Collection: Carstairs Gallery, New York.

References: Trente-six Bustes de H. Daumier, by Eugène Bouvy, Paris 1932, plate 23 from the original clay; "Bustes & Personages", by Charles Mourre, *Arts et Livres de Provence Number 8*, Marseille 1948, page 98. The author identifies the subject as a certain Falloux, saying: ". . . who became famous later on through his law on education, was only 22 years old the year the bust was modeled, but Daumier already gives him the look of an old man" (translation); *Daumier Sculpteur*, by Maurice Gobin, Paris 1952, catalogued number 23 as "Un Malin (inconnu) (unknown)", reproduced page 210, from the original clay page 211. Gobin disputes the identification of the subject as Falloux because of his age.

109 A

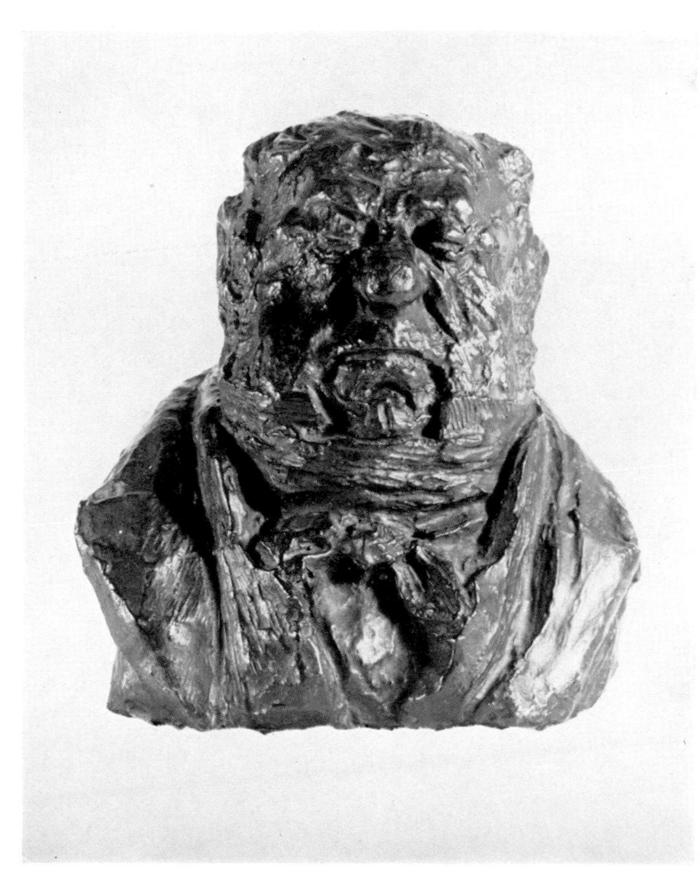

109 B

109 C

Honoré Daumier 1808-1879

110 LE RATAPOIL

Bronze, height 17½ inches

(1850)

Unsigned, stamped "Alexis Rudier, Paris Fondeur" *and* "6/20"

This, the most famous of Daumier's sculptures, portrays the same cynical and mercenary recruiting agent who appeared in so many of Daumier's drawings and lithographs. "The type is well-known – the raw-boned, half-starved, crafty soldier on half-pay. Topped by a crushed hat and wearing a military mustache and a menacing goatee, he stands erect on two lanky legs, his back arched under his worn frock coat, leaning on the thick stick which settles all arguments."[1]

"The statuette was executed prior to March of 1851, and, almost undoubtedly, around October of 1850, the date that Ratapoil makes his appearance in Daumier's lithographs (L. D. 2035). We know that Michelet, unacquainted with Daumier, went to visit him in his studio and 'fell on his knees' before him praising him for his 'admirable ability as a draughtsman, his genius as a thinker, his power to be just'. Then, seeing the statuette that Daumier was working on he cried in enthusiasm, 'Ah! You've caught the enemy now! That's it! The Bonapartist idea forever pilloried by you!'."[2]

[1] Maurice Gobin, *Daumier Sculpteur*, Geneva 1952, number 61, page 25. [2] Jean Adhémar, *Honoré Daumier*, Paris 1954, page 116, number 36.

Collection: Baron Henri Petiet, Paris.

References: Daumier, by Gustave Geffroy, Paris 1901, reproduced page 21; "Daumier Sculpteur", by Gustave Geffroy, *L'Art et Les Artistes*, Volume I, 1905, page 108; *Honoré Daumier*, by Erich Klossowski, 2nd Ed., Munich 1923, catalogue number 459, reproduced plates 10 and 11; *Daumier Peintre et Lithographe*, by Raymond Escholier, Paris 1923 reproduced page 152; *Der Maler Daumier*, by Eduard Fuchs, 2nd Ed., Munich 1930, mentioned page 52, number 171; *Daumier Raconté par lui-même et par ses amis*, Geneva 1945, reproduced page 161; *Daumier Sculpteur*, by Maurice Gobin, Geneva 1952, catalogued page 299, number 61 ter, reproduced pages 298 and 299; *Sculpture, Theme and Variations Towards a Contemporary Aesthetic*, by E. H. Ramsden, London 1953, Plate 24; *Honoré Daumier*, by Jean Adhémar, Paris 1954, Plate 36 and catalogued page 116, number 36; *Contemporary Sculpture*, by Carola Giedion-Welcker, New York 1955, reproduced page 3.

110

Hilaire Germain Edgar Degas 1834-1917

111 DANCER

Bronze, height 16¾ inches

(1896–1911)

Signed front right of base, "Degas", *and stamped back left of base,* "Cire Perdue A. A. Hébrard" *and* "51/K"

"The painting of Degas developed on a plan absolutely opposed to Renoir's. It brought him gradually to reduce his emphasis on line in painting in order to seek the pictorial. His last pastels are multicolored fireworks where all precision of form disappears in favor of a texture that glitters with hatchings. And yet Degas is the only one among all these painter-sculptors who brought to sculpture a more than an occasional or belated interest. At least since 1880 he devoted nearly as much time to modeling as to painting, or to his pastels or drawings. If the place this activity occupied in his life does not show up in his other works, if we do not observe in them that link which intimately unites the later paintings and sculptures of Renoir, it is precisely because Degas was not a painter who models nor a sculptor who paints. Even though nearly all his statuettes represent aspects of problems which sometimes pre-occupied the painter for long periods, even though the same postures of models are to be found in his paintings, pastels and drawings as well as in his statuettes, these last are never seen with the eyes of a painter or a draughtsman, they are conceived by a sculptor who seeks nothing but form." (John Rewald, *Degas Works in Sculpture,* New York 1944, page 2.)

Collection: Mlle. Jeanne Fevre (Niece of the Artist), Paris; Mme. A. Hébrard, Paris; Galerie Max Kaganovitch, Paris.

Exhibited: Galerie Max Kaganovitch, Paris, June 11–July 11, 1949; *Sculpture by Painters,* Curt Valentin Gallery, New York. November 20–December 15, 1952, number 22.

References: Degas Works in Sculpture. A Complete Catalogue, by John Rewald, New York 1944, page 26, number LII as "Dressed dancer at rest, hands behind her back, right leg forward", reproduced page 115; *Les Sculptures inédites de Degas. Choix de Cires Originales,* by Pierre Borel, Geneva 1949, reproduced (no pagination) from the original wax; *Degas et son Oeuvre,* by Paul André Lemoisne, Paris 1954, reproduced facing page 112; *Degas Sculpture,* by Leonard von Matt and John Rewald, New York 1956, catalogued page 153, number LII, reproduced plate 52; *Degas. Das plastische Werk,* by Leonard von Matt and John Rewald, Zürich 1957, catalogued page 157, number LII, reproduced plate 52.

111

Auguste Rodin 1840-1917

112 HEAD OF BALZAC

Bronze, height 7½ inches

(1893)

Signed at back right, "A. Rodin" *and stamped* "A. Rudier, Fondeur, Paris"

"Rodin is the father of modern sculpture, and probably the greatest sculptor of our day. While his principal work was done in the last quarter of the nineteenth century his influence on modern sculpture had probably been more profound than any other . . .

"However great the debt of the twentieth-century sculptor to the painter, his greatest single debt is to Rodin. Whether they were his studio assistants like Bourdelle and Despiau, or came under his direct influence like Brancusi, Matisse and Picasso, or derived from the same impressionist and expressionist traditions like Degas, Renoir, Rosso, Martini and Epstein, the power of his genius can be perceived in practically all the sculpture of our time . . ."[1]

"Modern Sculpture was to make a distinct contribution to the history of the art by the creation of a dynamic interplay of plane surfaces. I have already shown how Rodin introduced the notion of movement into his sculpture by an impressionistic trick . . . By using bronze with a reflective surface, this combination of roughness and smoothness produces a play of light that, as one moves around the object or moves the object around, gives animation to it; it seems to move itself."[2]

[1] Andrew Carnduff Ritchie, *Sculpture of the Twentieth Century*, New York 1952, pages 14 and 16. [2] Herbert Read, *The Art of Sculpture*, New York 1956, pages 97 and 98.

Collection: Curt Valentin Gallery, New York.

Exhibited: Auguste Rodin, Curt Valentin Gallery, New York, May 4–29, 1954, Number 26.

Reference: The Art of Sculpture, by Herbert Read, New York 1956, page 111, plate 190.

12

Henri Matisse 1869–1954

113 GRAND NU ASSIS (Seated Nude)

Bronze, height 16¾ inches

(1907–08)

Signed lower right rear, "H.M. 8/10" *and the founder's mark lower left rear,* "Cire Perdue C. Valsuani"

"Matisse produced rather little sculpture in 1908 and 1909 but two bronzes, the *Two Negresses* and *La Serpentine*, are among his best. A lesser piece, the *Seated Figure, Right Hand on Ground* . . . is modeled with a surface so ridged and gouged that even in the bronze one feels the wet plasticity of the clay. The figure is apparently a study for the much larger *Seated Nude* of about 1908." (Barr, *Matisse*, page 138.)

Collection: Curt Valentin Gallery, New York.

Exhibited: Sculpture by Painters, Curt Valentin Gallery, New York, November 20–December 15, 1951, number 50 as "Crouching Nude" and reproduced in the catalogue; *The Sculpture of Henri Matisse*, Curt Valentin Gallery, New York, February 10–28, 1953, number 19 and reproduced in the catalogue; *The Struggle for New Form*, World House Galleries, New York, January 22 – February 23, 1957, number 51 as "Crouching Nude".

References: New York Times, November 5, 1939, reproduced as "Seated Woman"; *Matisse: His Art and His Public*, by Alfred H. Barr, Jr., New York 1951, page 138.

114 TETE DE MARGUERITE

Bronze, height 12½ inches

(1915)

Signed lower right, "H.M. 4/10" *and the founder's mark lower left rear,* "Cire perdue C. Valsuani"

"Between 1900 and about 1912 Matisse produced over thirty pieces of sculpture, one or more practically every year. Then, excepting the tall narrow head of Marguerite in 1915 and three minor bronzes done at Nice about 1918, he stopped until 1925." (Barr, *Matisse*, page 217.)

Collection: Curt Valentin Gallery, New York.

Exhibited: The Sculpture of Henri Matisse, Curt Valentin Gallery, New York, February 10–28, 1953, number 28 and reproduced in the catalogue; *Closing Exhibition, Sculpture, Paintings and Drawings*, Curt Valentin Gallery, New York, June 1955, number 135 and reproduced in the catalogue; *Henri Matisse: Sculpture, Drawings*, Fine Arts Associates, New York, November 25 – December 20, 1958, number 17 and reproduced in the catalogue.

Reference: Matisse: His Art and His Public, by Alfred H. Barr, Jr., New York 1951, pages 213 and 217 and reproduced page 401.

113

114

Charles Despiau 1874-1946

115 DOMINIQUE (Mlle. D. Jeanès)

Bronze, height 14 inches

(1925)

Signed back left, "C. Despiau", *and stamped back left* "2" *and* "Cire perdue C. Valsuani"

"In 1903, he was 'discovered' by Rodin, with whom he collaborated on several works – among them the monument to Puvis de Chavannes.

"But the younger man discovered that his nature actually had little in common with Rodin's romantic and often sensual adventures in sculpture, his choice of 'titanic' subject matter, his reliance on bravura, and his, so often, preposterous titles ('The Hand of God' – as a single instance – which was the title for what is simply a 'blow-up' of a man's hand). So, after long consideration, the apprentice, who had learned that violence was not to be confused with power, bade his master farewell and thereupon embarked on an individual career."[1]

"Despiau's sculpture is not an art of compromise; on the contrary. But the artist introduces optical modifications into his compositions, which conceal the license he permits himself. This daring may not be obvious: it cannot be denied. A portrait by Despiau is primarily a sphere or a polyhedron. The features of the fore part of the head are interpreted as plastic forms. If the geometrical element is not apparent to the eye, it is because the artist is careful to conceal it. This caution should not deceive anyone. Charles Despiau, who knows so well the conformation of natural structures, has no desire to reduce them to cone or cylinder. But he does reveal to us those mysterious harmonies between the work of art and the organic body, with which Leonardo was continually preoccupied. 'He who can depict the human being,' wrote the old de Vinci, 'can depict the Universal.' The universality of such a sculptor as Despiau is to be found in his bronze heads whose suggestive power varies according to whether they seem to be speaking and alive to the outside world, or withdrawn into themselves, silent, struck by a kind of stupor. Among these faces are some like little works of architecture; others have something of a landscape."[2]

[1] Frank Crowninshield, "Despiau, Foremost Sculptor of our Time", *Vogue*, May 15, 1944, page 136. [2] Waldemar George, *Despiau*, London 1958, the 7th and 8th pages of the unpaginated text.

Collection: Frank Crowninshield, New York, from the artist.

References: "Charles Despiau, Essai sur l'Ame de la Sculpture", by Arsène Alexandre, *La Renaissance de l'Art Français*, February 1928, page 56, reproduced page 54; *C. Despiau*, by Léon Deshairs, Paris 1930, page 82, plate 32; *L'Art et les Artistes*, February 1932, reproduced on the cover.

115

Charles Despiau 1874-1946

116 L'ADOLESCENTE

Bronze, height 26½ inches

(1929)

Signed back right, "C. Despiau" *and stamped back left,* "2" *and* "Cire perdue C. Valsuani"

"His sculptures have repeatedly been described as *classical*; his male athletes and female nudes compared to those of the ancient Greeks. But, if we study them well, we can sense that they could only have derived from twentieth-century wellsprings, and from a spirit unmistakably French in its origin. It is true that his works, like those of the ancients, are serene, but it is a serenity which is, at the same time, endlessly and mysteriously astir. That quality in them is born not only of the artist's spirit, but of the spirit of the age in which he lives. And therein lies the paradox in Despiau's art; that his portraits, while dreaming, still, by some incalculable process of hypnosis, forever remain awake."[1]

"He shows a great repugnance for improvisation. He had no ease of manner. He required sixty sittings from his models. His method is purely empirical, and in principal at any rate, it excludes all preconceived ideas. It is based in the first place on observation; secondly on the knowledge inherited from the workers in plaster who were his forefathers. He flatters himself on the purity of his vision. He is quite alone before his lump of clay. No image, no memory, comes between him and his model."[2]

[1] Frank Crowninshield, "Despiau, Foremost Sculptor of our Time", *Vogue*, May 15, 1944, page 138. [2] Waldemar George, *Despiau*, London 1958, the 4th page of the unpaginated text.

Collection: Frank Crowninshield, New York, from the artist.

Exhibited: Twenty-nine Sculptures by Charles Despiau, Fifty-Sixth Street Galleries, New York, December 16–28, 1929, number 11 as "Diane"; *Modern European Art*, The Museum of Modern Art, New York, October 4–25, 1933; *Interpretations in Bronze*, Circulating Exhibition of The Museum of Modern Art, New York, 1948.

References: "Charles Despiau, Essai sur l'Ame de la Sculpture", by Arsène Alexandre, *La Renaissance de l'Art Français*, February 1928, page 59, reproduced page 57; *C. Despiau*, by Léon Deshairs, Paris 1930, plate 51; "Charles Despiau", by Agnes Rindge, *Parnassus*, March 1930, reproduced page 15 as "Diane"; "Charles Despiau", by Gustave Kahn, *L'Art et les Artistes*, February 1932, page 163 from the marble; *Art News*, January 1–14, 1942, reproduced page 22 *Charles Despiau* (The Arts Portfolio Series), New York, n.d.; *Despiau* by Adolphe Basler (Les Albums d'Art, volume 9), n.d., figure 2 from the plaster; "Interpretations in Bronze", *Art News*, September 1947, reproduced page 19; *The Museum of Modern Art Circulating Exhibition 1947-1948*, New York 1947, reproduced page 8.

Charles Despiau 1874-1946

117 MARIA LANI (With eyes open)

Bronze, height 14¼ inches

(1929)

Signed back left, "C. Despiau", *and stamped back right,* "2/8" *and* "Cire perdue C. Valsuani"

Despiau made two busts of Maria Lani, a famous model who sat for many painters and sculptors. One of the two portraits shows her with eyes lowered; this one with eyes open.

"Despiau's feeling for the early Greek, Egyptian, and Chinese sculptures is one of profound reverence. I recall that, a few years ago, he heard of a magnificent fourth-century, life-size Greek torso – critics had named Praxiteles as its author – which had come into the possession of a young friend of his. . . . Before, and after entering the room where the statue was exposed, he deliberately kept his eyes closed. Thus blinded, he proceeded, with every mark of pleasure, to run his sensitive, almost *seeing* fingers over the modeled surfaces of the marble, much as I have seen Helen Keller do with certain portraits by Jo Davidson.

"When Despiau finally opened his eyes, he gazed long and despairingly at the figure, and then turned to his young friend, saying, 'I must not, until nightfall, return to my studio. I might break every sculpture in it'."[1]

"Is there any sign of softening in Despiau's manner of execution? Certain planes, their edges blurred and indistinct, can hardly be perceived by the sense of touch. Faces, as those of Maria Lani, of Mrs. Charles Lindbergh, of Madame Pomerat, of Mademoiselle Bianchini seem to merge into the surrounding space, which gives the effect of an unreal halo. They belong to the realm of light and shade. The head of the actress Maria Lani seems to undergo strange metamorphoses. Her heavy eyelids tremble and blink. Her eyes open and close. Her cheeks draw in. Her lips move. Her forehead clouds over. In Despiau the myth of Pygmalion seems to live again. The passionate interest he brings to the study of the human personality prevents the artist from establishing a fixed canon. Despiau belongs to the moderns precisely because he prefers this search for a many-sided truth, of which he presents to us the relative aspect, to dogmas, formulae and authorities."[2]

[1] Frank Crowninshield, "Despiau, Foremost Sculptor of our Time", *Vogue*, May 15, 1944, page 138. [2] Waldemar George, *Despiau*, London 1958, the 8th page of the unpaginated text.

Collection: Frank Crowninshield, New York, from the artist.

Exhibited: A Show of Sculpture: Charles Despiau, Aristede Maillol, Institute of Modern Art, Boston, February 1–26, 1939, number 45.

References: "Charles Despiau", by A. H. Martinie, *L'Amour de l'Art*, November 1929, reproduced page 386; *C. Despiau*, by Léon Deshairs, Paris 1930, page 83, plate 44; "A Sculptor in Paris", by Ralph Nutall-Smith, *The Burlington Magazine*, September 1943, reproduced page 224, Figure A.

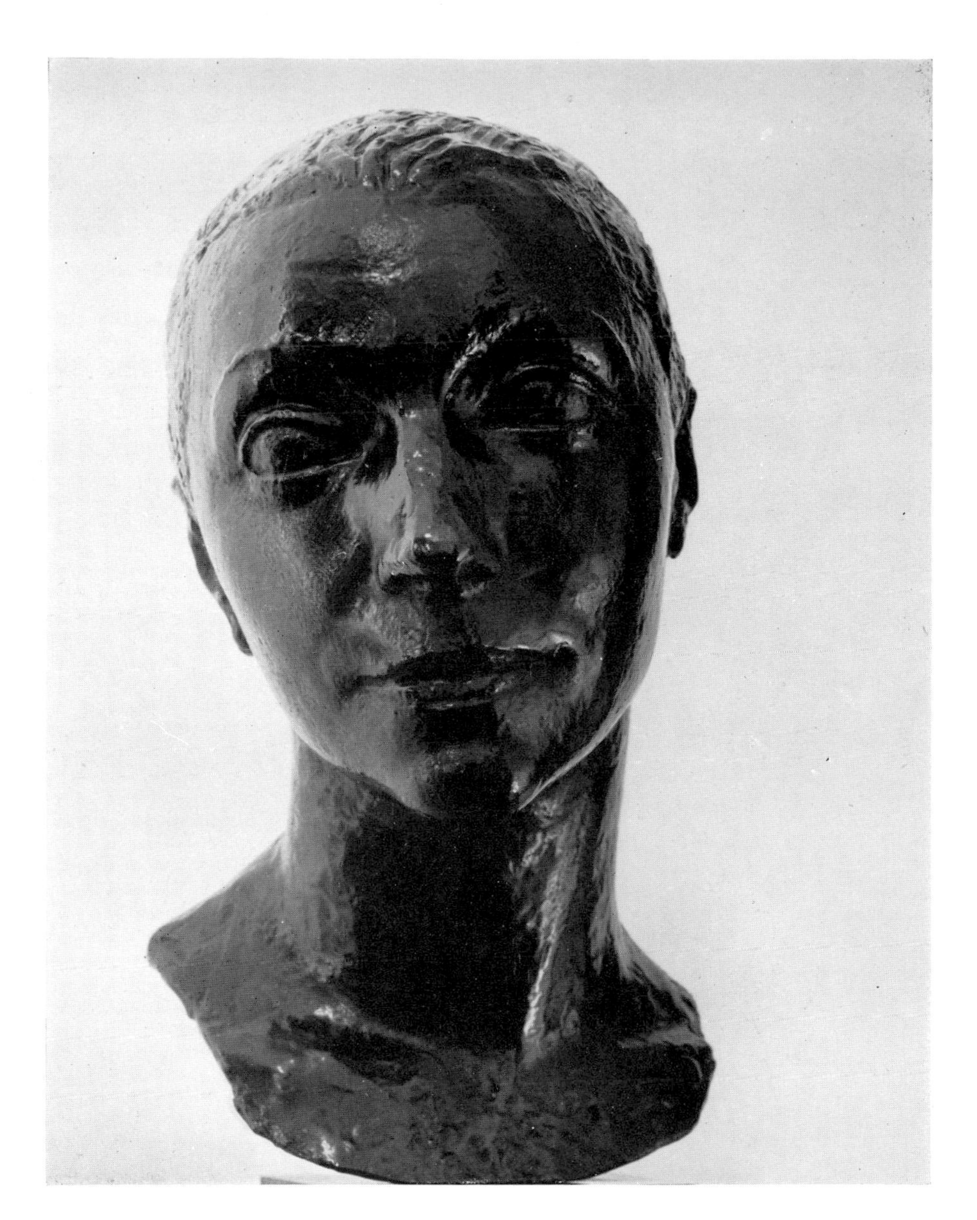

117

Charles Despiau 1874-1946

118 HEAD OF A GIRL: JACQUELINE

Bronze, height 14 inches

Signed back right, "2^{e} Epreuve C. Despiau"

"The style of Despiau is a kind of modernization of Rodin. It is as if by working down through the top layer of one of Rodin's brilliant busts we discovered the clear, convincing shape, rotund and truly constructed. From the particular standpoint of portraiture, in astuteness of characterization and suggestion of the way of life of the sitter, something is lost. When it is most beautiful, it conforms to a conception of French womanhood, serene and forceful and enigmatic. There is, perhaps, too marked a kinship between one face and another. Apparently Despiau cares more for this general beauty than for any particular reality, either physiological or psychological. But he is probably the most sought-after sculptor of portraits in the world and in the universal acceptance of his work, in spite of its austerity, we see how closely his ideal lies to our present sensibility."[1]

"Charles Despiau's works bear witness to the racial and intellectual origins of this Gascon whom Paris adopted. His Hellenism is not a trick of style, a constraint, nor is it a return to an earlier formula. It is a spiritual state. It is even the religion of the man. For the faces carved by Charles Despiau are the faces of women of the twentieth century. They have the same vibrant life, the sensitive intelligence, the lively expression of twentieth century woman. They are not Greek (nor Gothic) except in that they are human. Despiau, with those images of mortals and of the Olympic gods which he has bequeathed to posterity, belongs to the tradition of Christian atticism."[2]

[1] Monroe Wheeler, *20th Century Portraits,* New York 1942, page 29. [2] Waldemar George, *Despiau,* London 1958, the 4th and 5th pages of the unpaginated text.

Collection: Frank Crowninshield, New York, from the artist.

References: Mobilier & Décoration, November 1931, reproduced page 510; "Charles Despiau", by Gustave Kahn, *L'Art et les Artistes,* February 1932, reproduced page 172; *Auction Sale for the benefit of the United Hospital Fund,* M. Knoedler & Co., New York, December 9, 1947, number 8.

118

Constantin Brancusi 1876-1957

119 L'ORGEUIL (PRIDE)

Bronze, height 12 inches

(1907)

Signed side right, "C. Brancusi" *and stamped* "Cire perdue C. Valsuani"

"Brancusi's work unites the radiant formal beauty of the Mediterranean with an Oriental wisdom of form and symbolic power. It stands at the point of intersection of Eastern and Western civilization. No other sculptor of our day has achieved this fusion of sensuous understanding of all creaturely life with the supreme spiritualization of form. The essential shape, the universal significance of his forms, resides in their ultimate simplicity. They have reached perfection through the unremitting labor of the master's hand. The products of this slow process of creation stand in almost startling contrast to the rapid sculptural improvisations of Picasso, having left behind them all that is personal and contingent, and expressing a devout submergence of the individual in the universal." (Carola Giedion-Welcker, *Contemporary Sculpture*, New York, 1955, page 112.)

Collection: Curt Valentin Gallery, New York.

References: Cahiers d'Art, Volume 30, 1955 reproduced page 165 from the plaster; *Constantin Brancusi*, by Christian Zervos, Paris, 1957, reproduced page 21 from the plaster.

119

Jean Arp 1888-

120 CONCRETE SCULPTURE

White marble, height $14\frac{1}{8}$ inches

(1942)

Unsigned

" 'A one-man laboratory for the discovery of new form', Alfred Barr once called Jean (Hans) Arp. The description seems accurate when one considers the variety of Arp's plastic innovations in many media. At seventy-one his freshness of vision remains undiminished, and he works with the enthusiasm and boldness of his earlier career, creating sculptures in the round, bas-reliefs and those thoroughly original two-dimensional images which have extended in an important direction the vocabulary of art in our time. . . .

"The automatism of many of Arp's works has tended to obscure the importance of his capacity for acute observation in viewing the tangible world around him. The truth is that he is among other things a naturalist of the very finest order, stripping human and animal forms to a magic essence that far transcends realism to arrive at subtle evocations. . . . The word 'abstract' becomes almost meaningless when applied to some of Arp's sculptures, though the discipline of abstraction has engaged him persistently, notably in his many brilliant *collages*. And it must be added that Arp is one of the few contemporary artists whose contribution to psychological explorations has been just as important as his contribution to problems of formal order." (Soby, *Arp*, page 7.)

Collection: Curt Valentin Gallery, New York, from the *artist.*

Exhibited: Jean Arp, Buchholz Gallery, New York, January 18 – February 12, 1949, number 17, reproduced in the catalogue; *Jean Arp*, The Museum of Modern Art, New York, October–November 30, 1958, number 83, reproduced in the catalogue page 74.

Reference: Jean Arp, by Carola Giedion-Welcker, New York 1957, catalogued number 69 as "Concrete Form from Two Realms", reproduced page 75.

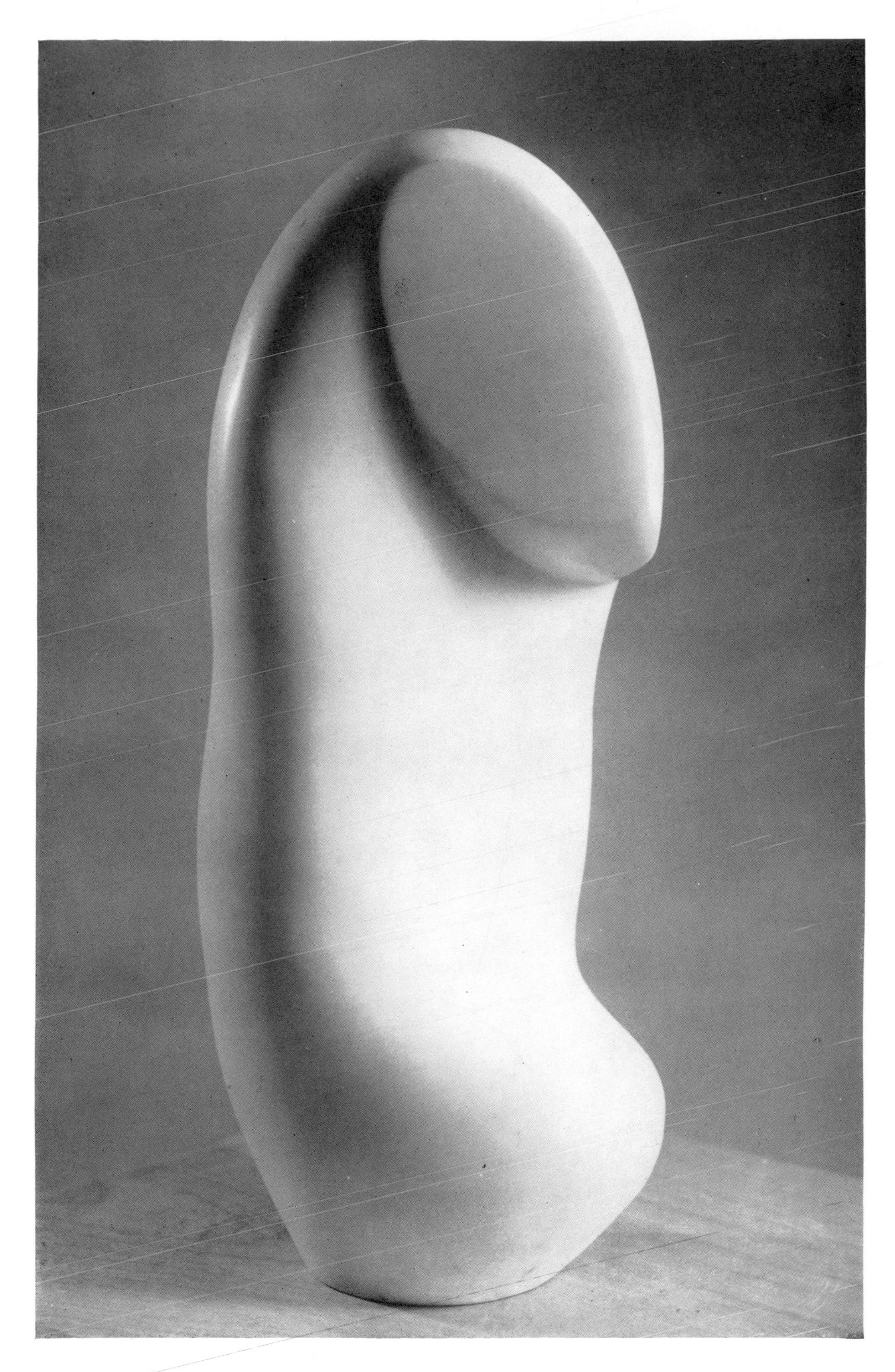

Jean Arp 1888-

121 NECKTIE IN SILENT TENSION

Black granite, height 8 inches, length 12 inches

(1947)

Unsigned

"One might say that Arp's regard for everyday objects is essentially metaphysical and that his aim is to restore to these objects their preternatural mystery. In this connection his art may be compared with some profit to that of the Surrealists who, following the example of Giorgio de Chirico, have disrupted the logic of ordinary associations by combining in their pictures objects of totally disparate meaning, so as to arrive at a provocative, new and unforeseen scenario derived from subconscious dictation. The difference, however, is obvious. Arp does not admire incongruity for its shock value. Rather his aim is to give a penetrating dignity to familiar forms both animate and inanimate, through a reappraisal of their metabolic capacity. Similarly, the 'double image', a persistent surrealist devise for obviating reality, has seldom if ever interested him. His statements about reality are unequivocal on the surface, but they revive a long-buried archaeology of the human spirit to which many other artists have since turned with profit and to which many more undoubtedly will turn in the future". (Soby, *Arp*, pages 8–9.)

Collection: Curt Valentin Gallery, New York, from the artist.

Reference: Jean Arp, by Carola Giedion-Welcker, New York 1957, catalogued number 88.

121

Jean Arp 1888-

122 CONFIGURATION IN SERPENTINE MOVEMENTS

White marble, height 9 inches, length 14 inches

(1950)

Unsigned

"Arp's symbolic language appears to express the principles of growth and continuous transformation that one finds in nature. Thus, he gives shape to the dreams of mankind. It is as if nature herself, and the circumstantial facts of physical existence, had formulated their own language of expression in the profound depths of consciousness. At the same time, all the types of form created by Arp are entirely independent of forms literally existing in nature; and they have been freed from limiting, specific detail. Particular form has become universal form, moving according to invisible forces within the cosmic scheme. Boldly, Arp fashions his image of the world in fragmentary symbols, enabling man to speak through nature, and nature through man. 'Arp's hypnotic language takes us back to a lost paradise, to cosmic secrets, and teaches us to understand the language of the universe', wrote Max Ernst, in comment upon the profound romanticism of his colleague's esthetic." (Carola Giedion-Welcker, "Arp: An Appreciation" in Soby, *Arp*, page 21.)

Collection: Curt Valentin Gallery, New York, from the artist.

Exhibited: Jean Arp, Curt Valentin Gallery, New York, March 2–27, 1954, number 8, reproduced in the catalogue; *The Struggle for New Form*, World House Galleries, (Opening Exhibit), New York, January 22–February 23, 1957, number 2; *Jean Arp*, The Museum of Modern Art, New York, October 6–November 30, 1958, number 94, reproduced page 97.

References: Jean Arp, by Carola Giedion-Welcker, New York 1957, catalogued number 109 as "Snake Movement I", reproduced page 84; "What isn't Art", *Time*, June 9, 1958, reproduced page 62.

122

Jean Arp 1888-

123 TORSO

White marble on polished black stone base, height 34⅝ inches

(1953)

Unsigned

"When Christopher Columbus, my pet, tried to sail to the East Indies 'the other way round', he discovered America. When we tried to paint 'the other way round', we discovered modern painting. It now seems incredible to me that I should have taken so long to realize that the art of our century and that of the preceding centuries are entirely different things. The beauty of Rembrandt's engravings, Giotto's frescoes, or the statuary of the Gothic cathedrals has little relation to the painting and sculpture of our day. They are as different from one another as the beauty of the nightingale's song and the beauty of the Gregorian chant. Even more so, in fact. They are incommensurable, like the beauty of the murmuring spring and the beauty of the rose, the beauty of a poem composed by the trees and the beauty of a snowflake." (Jean Arp in Soby, *Arp*, page 16.)

Collection: Curt Valentin Gallery, New York, from the artist: now the property of Smith College Museum, Northampton, Massachusetts, gift of Mr. and Mrs. Ralph F. Colin.

Exhibited: Jean Arp, The Museum of Modern Art, New York, October 6–November 30, 1958, number 98, reproduced in the catalogue page 98.

Reference: Jean Arp, by Carola Giedion-Welcker, New York 1957, catalogued number 120.

Not included in the exhibition at the Knoedler Gallery, April - May 1960.

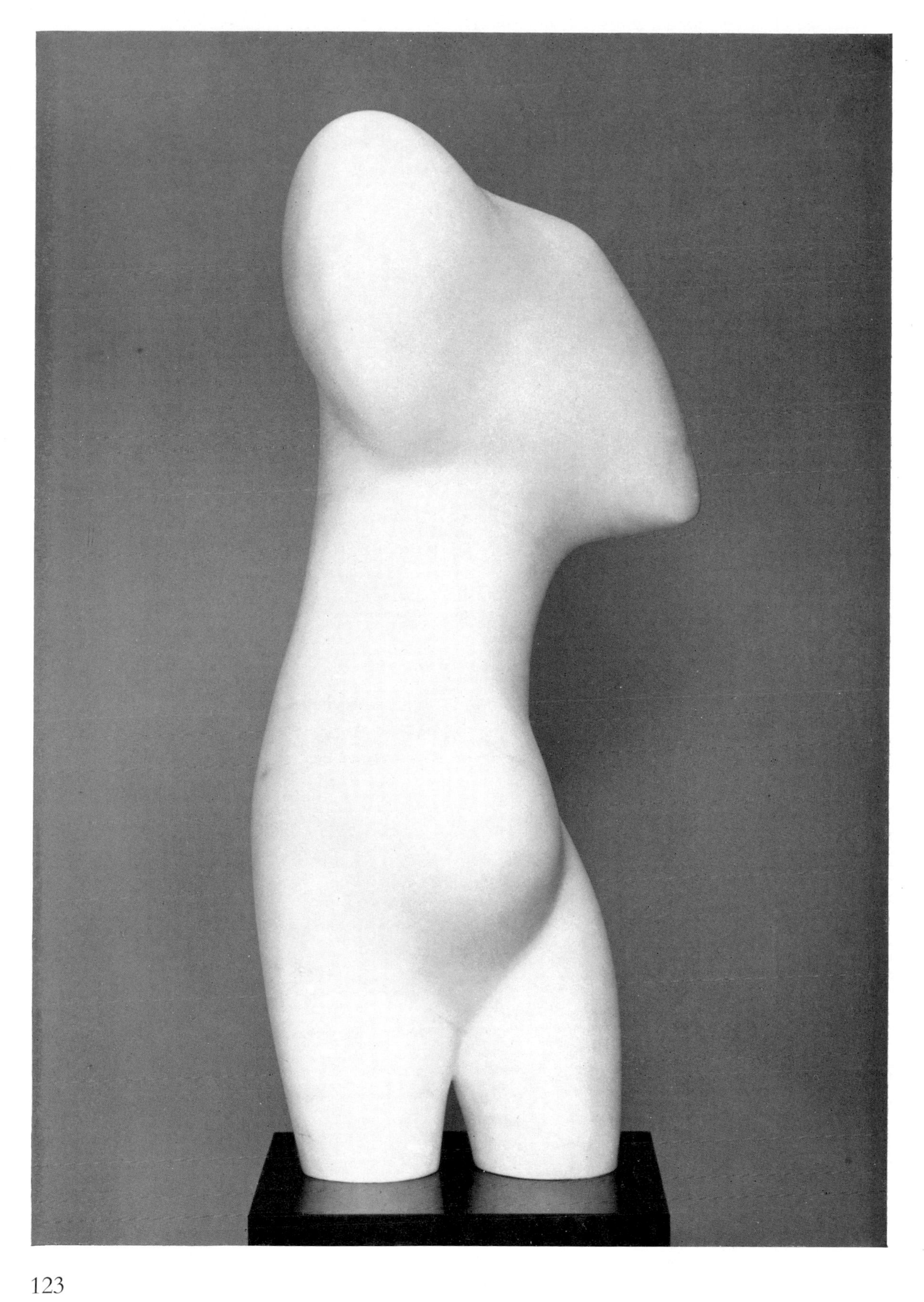

123

Jacques Lipchitz 1891-

124 SEATED BATHER

Pouillney stone, height 27½ inches

1917

Signed at the back, "J. L. 1917"

"In the grim atmosphere of war-time Paris [1915–18] Lipchitz went to work with a devotion and frugality that is reflected in the austerity of the new style . . .

"In the sculpture which followed, Lipchitz began to show his grasp of the cubists' analysis and penetration of form. His figures were represented as if seen from many angles and perspectives, often with a richly broken up surface of deep and shallow facets. . . . Yet the subordination of parts to whole, and the over-all effect of agitated movement, conflicting with the sheer, static mass of stone gives these sculptures a quality that is unique in cubist art.

"At this time his friendship with Juan Gris had brought Lipchitz into the inner circle of cubism . . .

"The interchange of ideas and images with others in the circle gave some of his work the collective quality of the movement. Occasionally his gouaches and polychromed reliefs, done mostly in 1918, resembled the work of the painters . . .

"But, always the sculptor, Lipchitz soon returned to his stone figures in the round. The group of clowns, musicians and bathers produced between 1917 and 1919 marks this period as one of the most brilliant in his career . . . They are images without explicit connotations; their beauty exists in the matter itself and its exciting configurations . . ."[1]

"*The Seated Bather*, 1917 (Fig. 3) and the *Reader*, 1918 (Fig. 4), return to the pathetic contraction of limbs and head so typical of figurative cubism. Both have the turning bend of the head, the arms held close to the body. They are built on a combination of curves and straight lines, with matching profiles and an answering rhythm of parts revolved through space, in accordance with the cubist concept of rhythmic repetition distributed through the whole and to the edges of the composition. In these works, for all their compact massiveness, something of the relief concept still remains; and for all their solidity, something of the shallow planar recession of cubist painting."[2]

[1] Henry R. Hope, *The Sculpture of Jacques Lipchitz*, New York 1954, pages 10 and 11. [2] Robert Goldwater, *Lipchitz*, London 1958.

Collection: Curt Valentin Gallery, New York, from the artist.

Exhibited: Jacques Lipchitz – Early Stone Carving and Recent Bronzes, Buchholz Gallery, New York, March 23–April 17, 1948, number 3 and reproduced in the catalogue; *Cubism*, Buchholz Gallery, New York, April 5–30, 1949, number 29 and reproduced in the catalogue; *Closing Exhibition. Sculpture, Painting and Drawings*, Curt Valentin Gallery, New York, June 1955, number 83.

Reference: Lipchitz, by Robert Goldwater, London 1958, reproduced plate 3.

124

Jacques Lipchitz 1891-

125 ACCORDION PLAYER

Bronze, height 25½ inches

(1917–19)

Signed, "J. Lipchitz"

"Lipchitz's recent sculpture is all curved outlines, modelled form and pierced volume; during those years of beginning it was composed of sharp edges, flat planes and solid mass. For the artist such alterations in appearance are trivial. This is partly because any style seems more varied and individual to its creators than it does from the unifying perspective of four decades distance. But more basically it is because 'cubism' must not be limited by the narrow terms of arbitrary period and external style. For Lipchitz cubism is a point of view, perhaps the point of view of the twentieth century. 'It is a vantage point,' he explains, 'which gave us all a new understanding of art and the world and their relation, and from which I still look down upon nature and the elements of creation.' Cubism is that break from the naturalist credo of the nineteenth century which restored to the artist his creative liberty, permitting him free play in the invention and arrangement of forms, allowing him maximum use of visual combination and imaginative association, loosening him from pedestrian concern with details, and making possible a wealth of allusive meaning through the interplay of created form.

"Lipchitz views the development of this essential freedom in historical perspective. He places its beginnings farther back than cubism and does not (as many other artists of his generation might) see its culmination in abstraction . . ."

Lipchitz is dissatisfied with abstraction, at least for his own art. "He admires the talent and sensitivity of many of the abstract sculptors of today, and his work – which is removed from realism of any kind – has made its contribution to the vision and techniques of abstraction. But he sees no necessary connection between abstraction and the twentieth century." (Robert Goldwater, *Lipchitz*, London 1958.)

Collection: Curt Valentin Gallery, New York, from the artist.

Exhibited: Closing Exhibition. Sculpture, Painting and Drawing, Curt Valentin Gallery, New York, June 1955, number 88 where it is dated 1926; *Art Our Children Live With*, The Downtown Gallery, New York, December 9–21, 1957, number 25.

125

Henry Moore 1898-

126 HEAD OF AN ANIMAL

Bronze, height 7¾ inches, length 11 inches

(1951)

Unsigned; one of eight casts

"In 1931, Jacob Epstein said, 'Henry Moore is the one important figure in contemporary English sculpture. If sculpture is truly the relation of masses then here is an example for all to see. Henry Moore by his integrity to the central idea of sculpture calls all sculptors to his side . . . Bound by the severest esthetic considerations, this sculpture is yet filled with the spirit of research and experiment. It contains the austere logic of ancient sculpture . . . Even the smallest works of Moore have an impressive and remote grandeur . . . Moore has that quality that can startle the unthinking out of complacency . . .'

"Fifteen years later [1946 – and it is still true in 1960] Moore is still the one important figure in contemporary English sculpture. But in the interval he has taken his place in the international forefront as well. For as an artist Moore has the courage, the craftsmanship and talent that match his personal sympathy, humility and integrity. And in spite of the maturity and individuality of his early production, Moore has grown in stature as a creative artist with every completed major work, and continues to grow"[1]

"The organization of the cell intrigues modern man more than Carlyle's hero worship; the genetic laws, the splitting of the atom, depth psychology more than classic humanism, theological dogma and ethics based on metaphysics. We live in an analytical age, and Moore, as a representative of this age, expresses it in all its aspects. Not Achilles, the Greek ideal, but the Warrior with Shield (ill. no. 28), the body of modern man mutilated by world wars, with a deep gash in his head, battered but proud and not succumbing to dread. The bone structure of living matter (ill. no. 20) rather than the myth of Amor and Psyche, the lower living organisms (ill. no. 17) rather than the Ecce Homo. How nature shapes cavities in cliffs or inside the muscular system in man and animal, how it withers rocks or smoothes pebbles – this is an example and a task for the modern sculptor."[2]

[1] James Johnson Sweeney, *Henry Moore*, New York 1946, page 88. [2] J. P. Hodin, *Moore*, London 1958.

Collection: Curt Valentin Gallery, New York, from the artist.

Exhibited: Henry Moore, Curt Valentin Gallery, New York, November 2 – December 4, 1954, number 2; *Closing Exhibition. Sculpture, Paintings and Drawings*, Curt Valentin Gallery, New York, June 1955, number 143.

References: Henry Moore. Volume Two. Sculptures and Drawings since 1948, London 1955, plates 30 and 30a; *Sculpture in Europe Today*, by Henry Schaefer-Simmern, Berkeley and Los Angeles 1955, plate 85; *Moore*, by J. P. Hodin, London 1958; *The Archetypal World of Henry Moore*, by Erich Neumann, New York 1959, page 120 and reproduced figures 96a, 96b and 96c; *Henry Moore*, by Will Grohmann, Berlin 1960, page 104 and reproduced plate 102.

126

Alberto Giacometti 1901-

127 CITY SQUARE (First Version)

Bronze, base 24¾ × 17; height of figures about 6½ inches, over-all height about 8½ inches

(1948)

Signed front right, "A. Giacometti" and stamped "2/6"

"Alberto Giacometti, who for the past twenty years has concentrated on the development of a linear sculpture, uses plastic line both to express movement and to create a conception of space. His early works in this medium, about 1932–34, were often in the form of 'projects' for a city square or 'place' and consisted of the outlines only of buildings with one or two symbols for human beings or birds suspended within the scaffolding. More lately Giacometti dispenses with the buildings and creates an impression of space simply by the disposition, on a platform, of linear symbols for human figures, instinct with movement. They seem to weave a concept of space by their indicated directions, which are opposed, away from each other. They do not seem to have a common center, and by this ambiguity they create an impression not of perceptual space but of metaphysical space."[1]

"Giacometti does not deal with the human group as it was understood by medieval artists and by Rodin in his *Burghers of Calais*, that is, as a whole, united from within through a common action and emotion. He is interested in the movement of the anonymous city-dweller both in his individual isolation and his collective relationships. The mysteriousness of everyday life, and the relationships of amorphous bodies in space that marked Giacometti's early work are now transformed into a counterpoint of moving human figures composed of little more than armatures. Everything is tense with movement and ravaged by space, and in this space, the human figure moves like a disembodied cipher. This work could not suffer a tactile approach since that would rob it of its mysterious tension in time and space. Very often Giacometti withdraws his figures from possible intimacy by interposing a pedestal and raising them into a spacial and spiritual zone of unreality. Their presence is submerged in dreamy remembrance; their intensity is psychic. They are parables of life, and they embody no actual event. They stand in complete contrast to Rodin's heroics, and are spiritually and formally more related to Medardo Rosso's anonymous groups."[2]

[1] Herbert Read, *The Art of Sculpture*, New York 1956, pages 102–3. [2] Carola Giedion-Welcker, *Contemporary Sculpture*, New York 1955, page 93.

Collection: Pierre Matisse Gallery, New York, from the artist.

References: Sculpture of the Twentieth Century, by Andrew Carnduff Ritchie, New York 1952, page 33, reproduced page 211; *Sculpture: Theme and Variations Towards a Contemporary Aesthetic*, by E. H. Ramsden, London 1953, plate 84b; *Contemporary Sculpture*, by Carola Giedion-Welcker, New York 1955, reproduced page 93; *The Art of Sculpture*, by Herbert Read, New York 1956, page 102 and plate 207; *Alberto Giacometti-Essais, Photos, Dessins*, by Ernst Scheidegger, Zürich 1958, reproduced page 108.

127

Marino Marini 1901–

128 HORSE AND RIDER

Bronze, height 18 inches

(1948)

Signed on back of base, "M. M."

"The important young sculptors . . . who have come up during and since the last war may be divided broadly into three groups. Those who are following the organic abstract tradition of Brancusi, Arp and Moore; those who are continuing the constructivist tradition; and, the most avant-garde of all, the so-called abstract expressionists who perhaps owe more to the metaphorical, symbolic and technical example of surrealists like Giacometti and Gonzalez than to any other one source.

"Outside these groups lie three of the leading Italian sculptors, Marini, Manzù and Fazzini. All three look back to the renaissance-derived expressionist tradition which Rodin, Rosso and Martini had established in their several ways . . . All are modelers by preference, and each displays a technical virtuosity which would have dismayed their futurist compatriot Boccioni, who detested mere virtuosity for its own sake. Of the three, Marini, despite his archaizing tendencies, is perhaps the strongest and most original talent. He has concentrated on a relatively limited number of motifs, the horse and rider, the female nude and portrait heads . . . " (Andrew Carnduff Ritchie, *Sculpture of the Twentieth Century*, New York 1952, page 34.)

Collection: Buchholz Gallery, New York from the artist.

Exhibited: Sculpture, Buchholz Gallery, New York, September 26 – October 14, 1949, number 33; *Marino Marini*, Buchholz Gallery, New York, February 14 – March 11, 1950, number 26; *Paintings by Mario Sironi with Sculpture by Marino Marini*, The Institute of Contemporary Art, Boston, April 30–June 6, 1953, number 61 and M. H. De Young Memorial Museum, San Francisco, June 19–July 19 and Colorado Springs Fine Arts Center, September 1–October 15 and Delaware Art Center, Wilmington, October 27–November 24; *20th Anniversary Exhibition 1936–1956*, The Institute of Contemporary Art, Boston, January 9–February 10, 1957, number 37.

Marino Marini 1901-

129 HORSE

Bronze, height 29½ inches

(1948)

Signed on base, "M. M."

"Marini's voice is one of the deepest and clearest in the newer European art scene. For many years he developed slowly, fighting facility harder than doubt, until a decade or so ago his true authority began. If his struggle has been arduous, it has left him tranquil and sure. 'To surmount the great accomplishments of the earlier twentieth century,' he says, 'temperament is possibly more necessary than intelligence.' His own temperament is unmistakably Tuscan (he was born in Pistoia and trained at the Academy in nearby Florence). But his closest affinities in Tuscan sculpture are with the pre-Mannerist epoch, before the control of massive form became subsidiary to linear invention. It is not Cellini, and it is not for that matter even Donatello, of whom he makes one think. It is the late thirteenth-century artist – was it Giovanni Pisano? – who created the marvelous evangelical bull now in the museum at Siena. This is not to say that Marini's sculpture is medieval in style, but only that its eagerness, awe and intuitive strength are paralleled in the art of a more innocent and spiritual time. It is no accident that, in addition to his other gifts, he should be perhaps the finest portraitist since Despiau. For Marini is as distinguished for his human warmth as for his resolution of the more abstract sculptural problems. 'I should like', he says simply, 'to defend for humanity its form'."[1]

"To be an artist is simple. It is simplicity which is difficult. In Italy so much is truly simple – the land, the people. Our discipline is not that of the North; it is far less intellectual."[2]

[1] James Thrall Soby in introduction to the Marini exhibition catalogue, Buchholz Gallery, New York 1950.
[2] Marino Marini in *op. cit. supra.*

Collection: Buchholz Gallery, New York, from the artist.

Exhibited: Marino Marini, Buchholz Gallery, New York, February 14–March 11, 1950, number 21 and reproduced in the catalogue; *Summer Loan Show,* The Metropolitan Museum of Art, New York, July–August 1950; *Festival of Art,* for the benefit of Federation of Jewish Philanthropies of New York, Waldorf-Astoria Hotel, October 29 – November 1, 1957, number 113.

Reference: Sculpture in Europe Today, by Henry Schaefer-Simmern, Berkeley and Los Angeles 1955, plate 26 where it is dated 1942.

129

Dorothy Dehner 1908-

130 RIVER LANDSCAPE

Bronze, $11\frac{1}{2} \times 27$

1958

Signed upper right, "Dorothy Dehner '58"

"Dorothy Dehner and David Slivka have engaged in calmer, more lucid approaches to similar problems. In their works, wit is permitted to lighten the mood. And the shapes themselves are kept relatively abstract – even when they suggest . . . a mythological landscape or construction in Miss Dehner's [bronzes]. She intuits the configuration of the environment necessary for an art of magic or a moment of contemplation . . . Miss Dehner's sensitivity to the medium gives her bronzes an air of luminosity and sensibility . . . Miss Dehner's bronzes look wonderfully complete. Where she makes an open space, it is filled to the brim by the life of the sculpture itself – as your lungs seem filled by a deep breath." (Thomas B. Hess, "U.S. Sculpture: Some Recent Directions", *Portfolio including Art News Annual Number 1*, New York 1959, pages 146 and 148.)

Collection: Willard Gallery, New York, from the artist.

Exhibited: Dehner Bronzes, Willard Gallery, New York, February 3–28, 1959.

Reference: "U.S. Sculpture: Some Recent Directions" by Thomas B. Hess, *Portfolio including Art News Annual Number 1*, New York 1959, pages 146 and 148, reproduced page 119.

130

Reg Butler 1913-

131 STUDY FOR GIRL WITH CHEMISE

Shell bronze, height 18½ inches

(1954)

Unsigned

"Reg Butler's forms are basically human and like the human frame they are hollow. His earlier figures existed as linear shapes in wrought iron, united by interpenetration of the essential elements of their structure. More recently his mastery of other mediums leads him to present us with surfaces which hide the inner void but still leave us conscious of vital forms within. There is continuous play between the receptive aspects cavernous interiors, limbs, like radar antennae, stretching towards invisible and inaudible waves and the aggressive fullness of form, ready to penetrate like a battering ram.

"The figures are not solidly based on earth but practice levitation. They are airborne and the upward gaze of their taunt, phallic heads lifts them even further from the ground, raising them in the imagination to the dimensions of inter-stellar space.

"By its sense of scale Reg Butler's work often suggests monumental proportions . . . Without employing unwieldy dimensions, he can make us feel the weight of a mass tugged downward by gravity and threatening to crush us like ants or force us to swing helplessly with his tortured but recognizably female figures, straining at their guide lines and writhing on the spears by which they are impaled . . ." (Roland Penrose in catalogue of Reg Butler Exhibition, Curt Valentin Gallery, New York, January 11–February 15, 1955.)

Collection: Curt Valentin Gallery, New York, from the artist.

Exhibited: Reg Butler, Curt Valentin Gallery, New York, January 11–February 15, 1955, number 38, reproduced in the catalogue.

Reference: Art News, February 1955, reproduced page 59.

131

Reg Butler 1913-

132 FIGURE IN SPACE

Bronze, height $9\frac{7}{8}$ inches, length 20 inches

(1956)

Unsigned

"It is, I am convinced, a profound mistake, to approach an understanding of art through assessments of whether it is 'true', or 'false' – whether or not it 'represents'. For, most of all a sculpture is the mark a man makes on the walls of his cell to consume his boredom or assuage his fear; to expiate his guilt or simply to record the passing of his time. The marks are what they are and not in any important sense a proposition about . . .

"Naturally, in a secondary sense, information may be gathered about the artist's mind from an examination of his mark; and further, about the society of which he is part. But deductions of this kind, while of interest to psychologists and sociologists are beside the point aesthetically.

"The aesthetic question is alone the peculiar province of art, and the plain fact is that some men make ugly marks and others beautiful marks; and the question which links the artist, the work and the observer is heavily loaded with subjectivity at both ends.

"What therefore, believing this, can I say about my own work? Very little, except that it is my mark, my autobiography; and that to some extent, it may be part of the biography of my time . . . that the degree in which it may be more than a purely local and personal mark will be the true measure of its success or failure." (Extract from a letter from Reg Butler to Pierre Matisse, dated January 1959, in catalogue of Reg Butler Exhibition, Pierre Matisse Gallery, New York, February 1959.)

Collection: Pierre Matisse Gallery, New York, from the artist.

Exhibited: Reg Butler, Sculpture and Drawings 1954 to 1958, Pierre Matisse Gallery, New York, February 1959, number 14, reproduced in the catalogue.

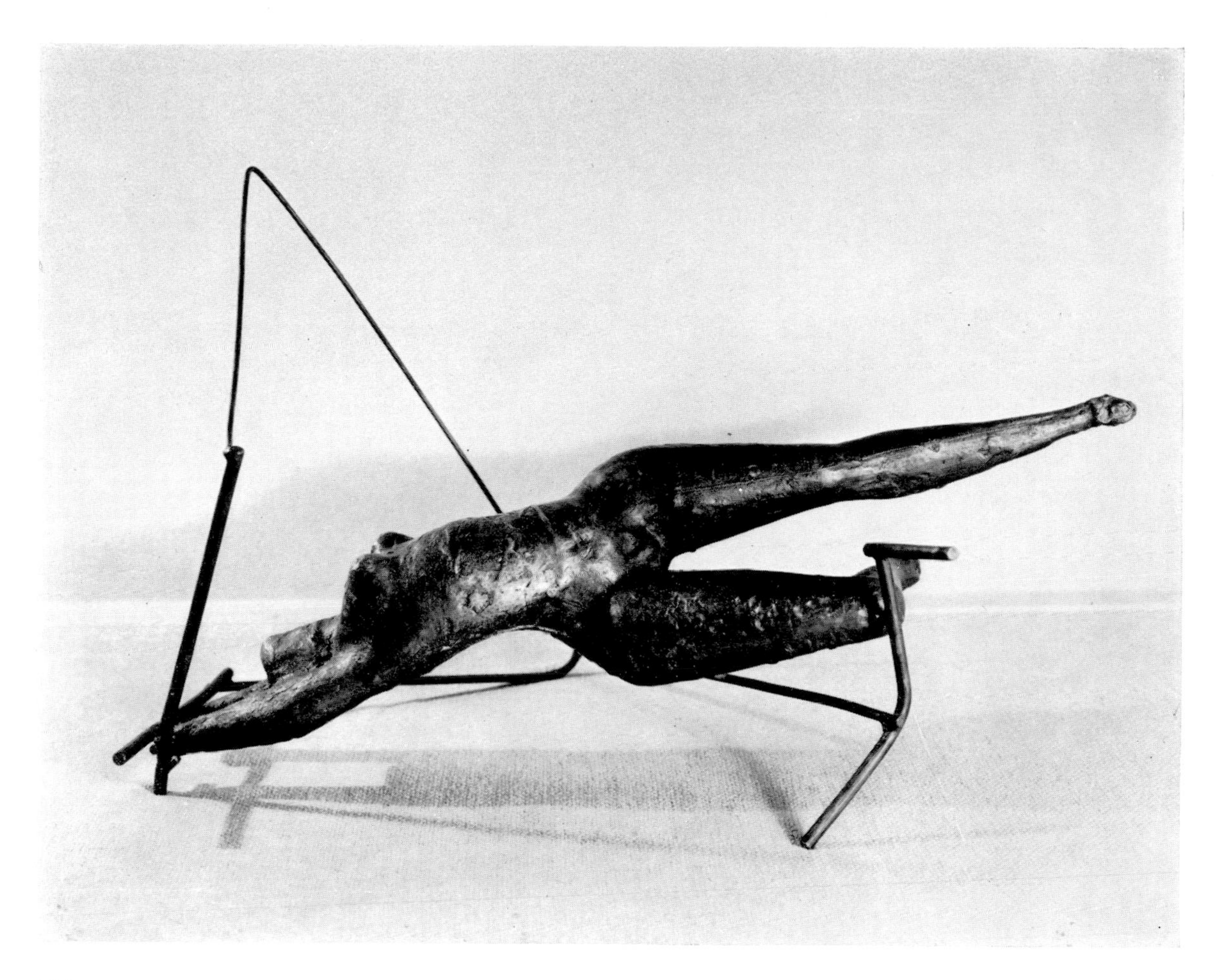

132

Three thousand copies of this catalogue of

THE COLIN COLLECTION

prepared by Ralph F. Colin

were printed in March 1960 by W. S. Cowell Ltd

at their press in the Butter Market, Ipswich, England.

Almost all the black and white photographs

were taken in New York by Suichi Sunami.

Other photographs were taken by

Adolph Studly, Oliver Baker, Brenwasser, and Herbert Loebel

all of New York.